Inspiration
&
Motivation

Alfred Armand Montapert

PRENTICE-HALL, INC.   Englewood Cliffs, N.J.

Prentice-Hall International, Inc., *London*
Prentice-Hall of Australia, Pty, Ltd., *Sydney*
Prentice-Hall of Canada, Ltd., *Toronto*
Prentice-Hall of India Private Ltd., *New Delhi*
Prentice-Hall of Japan, Inc., *Tokyo*
Prentice-Hall of Southeast Asia Pte. Ltd., *Singapore*
Whitehall Books, Ltd., *Wellington, New Zealand*

Library of Congress Cataloging in Publication Data
Montapert, Alfred Armand.
  Inspiration & motivation
  1. Quotations, English. I. Title. II. Title:
Inspiration and motivation.
PN6081.M518   082   81-23459
                                 AACR2
ISBN 0-13-467605-X

Printed in the United States of America

14114

PREFACE

THE HALL OF WISDOM

In my home I have a hall lined with hundreds of solid walnut and bronze plaques. Over half are my own sayings; the rest are the favorite trenchant sayings of others which I have incorporated into my life.

In sharing all the sayings on the plaques in my Hall of Wisdom, I share my ideals and philosophy which helped me enhance the quality of my life and achieve my goals in life. Each plaque saying was like a tile in a great mosaic that formed the picture of a happy, beneficial life. Today I am in a preferred position.

These trenchant sayings took a lifetime to gather. They will help you build your inner life. They help form your thoughts and beliefs, your high ideals and your philosophy. They give you strength, encouragement, and inner joy. They build the inner person. That means character, goodness, love, kindness, and the generous qualities.

They are the seeds that produce the inherent quality and values of a beautiful person ... providing you incorporate them into your life. Make them yours ... for they are beneficial, and your real wealth.

This book is designed for successful living. There is no need to lament the modern world. The *today* it offers is the only one we have and we must learn to make the most of it. We must learn to live with the problems and absurdities we now face; even use them to make a good living for ourselves and our families.

I want all my readers to love reality; ideally to be a lover of life ... a bon vivant!

Read on ... and may you be happy, healthy, and successful.

—*Alfred A. Montapert*

INTRODUCTION

This treasury of inspiration and real-life wisdom, selected by an eminent businessman and author of practical philosophy, offers the modern reader inspiring selections from many sources on successful living.

Here you will find thoughts and ideas for happiness, confidence and strength for living today and hope for the future...words that guide you to joyful living and help you perk along life's highway to contentment and satisfaction.

Bonaro W. Overstreet admonishes, *"If I can line up the people who back through the ages have gone at life in ways I greatly admire, then I can feel all their strength supporting me, all their standards and values pointing the way in which I am to go."* No man is wise enough by himself. Listen to the wise sage of England, Benjamin Disraeli: *"Nurture your mind with great thoughts."*

A great American, Ray Lyman Wilbur, speaks out: *"It is not how much you know about life, but how you live your life that counts. Those who can avoid mistakes by observing the mistakes of others are most apt to keep free from sorrow. In a world full of uncertainties, the record of what has gone before...human experience is as sure and reliable as anything of which we know."*

As you read through the pages of this book, you will meet some of the greatest men and women who ever walked on the face of this earth. I hope you meet a lot of your old friends. A friend looks out for his friend.

"To enhance the quality of the day—That is the highest of Arts."

—Thoreau

Here are the noblest and finest ideas of the world's greatest men throughout history ... in their own words ... about LEARNING ... LIVING ... and ACHIEVING.

To build a man or woman is the greatest project and the most rewarding business in this world ... for each of us! And the genius of man through the ages can be found in his most insightful moments ... in those flashes of great inspiration and aptness of thought ... in the keenest perceptions of the greatest thinkers and doers.

The purpose of this little volume is to enrich, ennoble, encourage you on your voyage through life. Here are verses of wisdom to give you guidelines to the abundant life we all seek.

The motivators and thought conditioners set forth in the following pages, when practiced, will help give you the power to achieve whatever goals you pursue. Positive thought reinforces positive response. Towards this end this book is dedicated.

YOU!

The environment YOU fashion out of
.... YOUR THOUGHTS ... YOUR BELIEFS....
... YOUR IDEALS... YOUR PHILOSOPHY ...
.... IS THE ONLY CLIMATE YOU WILL
EVER LIVE IN.

—*Alfred A. Montapert*

TABLE OF CONTENTS

ACKNOWLEDGMENT

Down through the centuries, the choice ideas of men and women who have gathered inspiration and truth from the fires of experience, and achieved knowledge in the pain and struggle, have left us a legacy of trenchant thoughts and have put their feelings into words.

HERE ARE GREAT THOUGHTS TO LIVE BY

We are heirs of all that man has ever dreamed, thought out, fought and died for ... all that he has eloquently written, or expressed, and left behind for the guidance of future generations. Many of these inspirations are from ordinary human beings who have worked out a formula for happy, successful living.

The author is proud of his Hall of Wisdom and shares all the greatest thoughts he has gathered throughout his lifetime as his legacy to the people of all the world. He knows that it will add years of knowledge and inspiration to the reader's life, and greatly enhance his or her personal effectiveness.

You will find something here for every mood and for every need.

Every generation enjoys the use of a vast hoard of wisdom, bequeathed to it by antiquity, and transmits that hoard, augmented by fresh acquisitions, to future ages.

—*Thomas Macaulay*

★ ★ ★

CHAPTER 1

INSPIRATION

Enthusiasm . . . . *Imagination* . . . . *Dreams*

INSPIRATION

A teacher who is attempting to teach without inspiring
the pupil with a desire to learn, is hammering on cold iron.

—*Horace Mann*

★ ★ ★

OPPORTUNITY

THE PASSING HOURS, DAYS AND YEARS
BRING OPPORTUNITIES WHICH QUICKLY PASS.
GRASP THEM NOW—OR LOSE THEM.

—*Alfred A. Montapert*

★ ★ ★

ENTHUSIASM

A man will succeed
at anything
about which he is
really enthusiastic.

—*Charles M. Schwab*

★ ★ ★

GLAD DAY

This is the day
the Lord has made...
I will rejoice
and be glad in it.

—*Psalms 118:24*

FRIEND

A FRIEND IS A PERSON . . . .

... With whom you can be sincere.

... To whom you never need to defend yourself.

... On whom you can depend whether present or absent.

... With whom you never need pretend.

... To whom you can reveal yourself without fear of betrayal.

... Who does not feel he owns you because you are his friend.

... Who will not selfishly use you because he has your confidence.

I WOULD HAVE SUCH A FRIEND ... AND I WOULD BE SUCH A FRIEND.

—Alfred A. Montapert

★ ★ ★

INSPIRATION

My greatest inspiration is a challenge
to attempt the impossible.

—Albert A. Michelson

★ ★ ★

YOUR BEST

EACH DAY MAKE IT A CHALLENGE
TO DO YOUR BEST ... LIVE YOUR BEST ...
For today will soon be tomorrow,
And tomorrow will soon be forever.

—The Way to Happiness

★ ★ ★

GREAT EXPECTATIONS

SOMETHING GREAT AND WONDERFUL
IS HAPPENING TODAY,
AND I AM A PART OF IT.
—Dr. Robert Scott

★ ★ ★

ASPIRATION

Hitch your wagon to a star.
—R. W. Emerson

★ ★ ★

TRUST

All that I have seen
teaches me to trust the Creator
for what I have not seen.
—R. W. Emerson

★ ★ ★

SUCCESS...

In its broadest definition...
OBEY GOD!
—Alfred A. Montapert

★ ★ ★

DISCIPLINE

If you are going to soar
with the eagles
in the morning,
you can't
hoot with the owls all night.
—Anon.

★ ★ ★

THE WAY

Show me the way—
  Not to fortune or fame,
Not how to win laurels
  Or praise for my name—
But show me the way
  To spread the Great Story
That *"Thine is the Kingdom
  and Power and Glory."*

—*Helen Steiner Rice*

* * *

MY DAILY GOAL

Try to improve...
The quality of each day...
And live mindful of...
How brief your life is.

—*Alfred A. Montapert*

* * *

HAPPY DAYS

"Very little is needed to make a happy life.
It is ALL within yourself...
In your WAY of thinking!"

—*Marcus Aurelius*

* * *

INSPIRATION

"Employ your time in improving yourself by other men's
writings, so that you shall come more easily by what others
have labored hard for."

—*Socrates*

* * *

EVERYTHING IS LOVELY

Sunshine is delicious, rain is refreshing,
wind braces us up, snow is exhilarating,
There is no such thing as bad weather,
only different kinds of good weather.

—John Ruskin

★ ★ ★

DREAMS

The greatest achievement was, at first and for a time, a
dream. The oak sleeps in the acorn; the bird waits in the egg;
and in the highest vision of the soul, a waking angel stirs.
Dreams are the seedlings of realities.

—James Allen

★ ★ ★

DEEDS

Our chief want in life
is somebody who shall make us
DO what we can.

—Emerson

★ ★ ★

"WELL DONE IS BETTER
THAN WELL SAID."

—Benjamin Franklin

★ ★ ★

PEACE OF MIND

Quiet minds cannot be perplexed or frightened but go
on, in fortune or misfortune, at their own pace, like a clock
during a thunderstorm.

—Robert Louis Stevenson

ASK YOURSELF

If TIME and MONEY and CIRCUMSTANCES
were no problem, what would you
like to do with the one life
you have to LIVE?

—Alfred A. Montapert

★ ★ ★

ADVANTAGE

In the land of the Blind,
The one-eyed man is King.

—Erasmus

★ ★ ★

VICTORY

A Victory without danger
Is a triumph without glory.

—Pierre Corneille

★ ★ ★

JUST A LITTLE NUT

The Great Oak
Was Once
A Little Nut
Who Held
Its Ground

—Grovenor Montapert

★ ★ ★

PATIENCE

Patience is the Companion
of Wisdom.

—St. Augustine

DREAMS

We grow great by dreams. All big men are dreamers. They see things in the soft haze of a spring day or in the red fire of a long winter's evening. Some of us let these great dreams die, but others nourish and protect them; nurse them through bad days till they bring them to the sunshine and light which comes always to those who sincerely hope that their dreams will come true.

—Woodrow Wilson

★ ★ ★

COMPETITION

Anybody can win
—unless—
there happens to be a
second entry.

—George Ade

★ ★ ★

MANKIND

Man is but a reed...
Nature's feeblest;
BUT HE IS A THINKING REED.

—Pascal

★ ★ ★

WISHFUL THINKING,

Be not angry...
that you cannot make OTHERS
as you wish them to be...
since you cannot even make YOURSELF
as you wish to be.

—Thomas à Kempis

★ ★ ★

SUCCESS

SUCCESS IS DEPENDENT ON EFFORT.

—Sophocles

★ ★ ★

AUTHORSHIP

The hand that guides the pen
Is as valuable as the hand
That guides the plough.

—Arthur Rimbuad

★ ★ ★

GIFTS

God gives everyone a bundle of Gifts.
It is what YOU DO with them that counts.

—Alfred A. Montapert

★ ★ ★

DO GOOD

If I can stop one heart from breaking,
I shall not live in vain;
If I can ease one life the aching,
Or cool one pain,
Or help one fainting robin
Unto his nest again,
I shall not live in vain.

—Emily Dickinson

★ ★ ★

ELOQUENCE

True eloquence comprises saying
all that needs to be said,
and only that.

—Francois de la Rochefocauld

SALUTATION

How's your FAITH?

—*Old New England Greeting*

* * *

CULTURE

POLITENESS
IS THE CHIEF INGREDIENT
OF CULTURE

—*Anon.*

* * *

CONDUCT

You are looking for the best rule for life—
Here it is:
To maintain a cheerful disposition;
To do and say what is right.

—*Latin*

* * *

BRAVE

The brave venture anything.

—*Euripides*

* * *

FAITH

In planning our life
And in our performance,
We have the resources
Of an omniscient and
An Almighty God.

—*Charles "Tremendous" Jones*

* * *

OVERCOME

IF WE ARE INTENDED FOR GREAT PURPOSES, WE ARE
EXPECTED TO OVERCOME GREAT TRIALS.

—Alfred A. Montapert

★ ★ ★

ENJOY LIFE

Don't worry,
don't hurry,
and don't forget to take time
to smell the flowers.

—Charles "Tremendous" Jones

★ ★ ★

ADMIRATION

All things are admired
either because they are new
or
because they are Great.

—Bacon

★ ★ ★

WISDOM

THE WISDOM OF LIFE
IS THE ELIMINATION
OF THE NON-ESSENTIALS

—Distilled Wisdom

★ ★ ★

SIMPLICITY

Simplicity is the badge
of Distinction and Genius.

—Alfred A. Montapert

INDIVIDUAL

The greatest things are accomplished
by individual people,
NOT BY COMMITTEES OR COMPANIES.

—*Alfred A. Montapert*

★ ★ ★

CHARACTER

Even when a bird walks
We see that it has wings.

—*Lemoine*

★ ★ ★

DOER versus TALKER

The world judges you by what you have done;
not by what you started out to do...
BUT BY WHAT YOU HAVE COMPLETED.
BE A DOER ... NOT A TALKER.

—*Alfred A. Montapert*

★ ★ ★

DON'T GIVE UP

DON'T GIVE UP ... KEEP LOOKING UP!
LOOK TO GOD,
THE SOURCE OF YOUR TOTAL SUPPLY.

—*Oral Roberts*

★ ★ ★

A GOOD NAME

"A GOOD NAME is rather to be chosen
than great riches ... and loving favour
rather than silver or gold."

—*Solomon*

PATIENCE

"LET US NOT BE WEARY
IN WELL-DOING:
FOR IN DUE SEASON
WE SHALL REAP
IF WE FAINT NOT."

—*Galatians 6:9*

★ ★ ★

IMAGINATION

What the mind of man
can conceive and believe,
it can ACHIEVE.

—*Jules Verne*

★ ★ ★

REALITY

REALITY is NOT the way you wish things to be,
But the way they actually are.
To be happy we must face REALITY.

—*Alfred A. Montapert*

★ ★ ★

ATTITUDE

Our ATTITUDE is extremely important; we become
what we dwell upon. If we dwell on adverse conditions, we
intensify the bad. A man will remain a rag-picker as long as
he has only the vision of the rag-picker. Think well of
yourself ... look on the sunny side of everything ... talk
health, happiness and prosperity to every person you meet.

—*Supreme Philosophy of Man*

★ ★ ★

FACTS COUNT

Facts are facts...
and will not disappear
on account of your likes or dislikes.
Not speech ... but FACTS convince.

—Alfred A. Montapert

* * *

BLESSINGS

Reflect upon your present blessings,
of which every man has many;
Not on your past misfortunes,
of which all men have some.

—Charles Dickens

* * *

GOODNESS

Not too much time remaining, Lord,
So let us use it well for Thee.
May we truly have a good account to give
for every year that You have let us live.

—Alfred A. Montapert

* * *

TRUE PLEASURE

The only TRUE PLEASURE is the pleasure
of creative activity.

—Tolstoy

* * *

PURPOSEFUL LIVING

What is the use of living if it be not to strive for noble causes
and to make this muddled world a better place to live in after
we are gone.

—Winston Churchill

BLESSINGS

Count your many blessings...
name them one by one.

—*J. Oatman*

★ ★ ★

A FRIEND

A friend is one who:
Pushes you in the swing,
Pulls you up the ladder,
Pats you on the back,
And hugs you good-bye.

—*Katherine N. Davis*

★ ★ ★

SEEKERS

We search the world for truth. We cull
The good, the true, the beautiful,
From gravestone and from written scroll
And all old flower-fields of the soul.

And, weary seekers of the best,
We come back laden from our quest
To find that all the sages said
Is in THE BOOK our mothers read.

—*John Greenleaf Whittier*

★ ★ ★

ENCOURAGEMENT

ENCOURAGEMENT IS OXYGEN TO THE SOUL.

—*Alfred A. Montapert*

★ ★ ★

PATIENCE

With age I have become more patient!

—*Eleanor Roosevelt*

LIVE

LIVE so enthusiastically you cannot fail.

—*Dorthea Brande*

* * *

ENTHUSIASM

"Give me men with fire in their bowels."

—*Oliver Cromwell*

* * *

BELONG TO YOURSELF

The great French essayist, Michel de Montaigne, retired at the tender age of thirty-eight. He wrote this good advice.

"I did not flee from men, but from affairs. We have lived long enough for others; let us live the rest for ourselves. Let us disentangle ourselves from the clutch of things which hold us elsewhere and keep us from ourselves. The greatest thing in the world is to know how to belong to yourself."

Don't follow the herd, they will take you out into the woods and lose you.

—*Alfred A. Montapert*

* * *

LIFE

The great object of living
is to attain more life...
More in QUALITY as well as QUANTITY.
Life will do a lot of growling...
But no one can hurt you except yourself!

—*Alfred A. Montapert*

* * *

DREAM

"Some men see things as they are and say, WHY?
Others dream things that never were and say, WHY NOT?"

—*Aeschylus*

★ ★ ★

KINDNESS

Struggle diligently against your impatience,
and strive to be friendly and gentle,
in season and out of season, toward everyone,
however much they may vex and annoy you.
And be sure God will bless your efforts.

—*St. Francis de Sales*

★ ★ ★

WORRY

Why take ye thought of food and raiment?
Consider the lilies, they are not busily engaged in toiling and
spinning. The birds of the air build no barns or storehouses,
neither do they sow, yet the Heavenly Father looketh after
them, mindful of their every need. Ten thousand times IN
ten thousand ways, many of which we are not even aware of,
God has showered goodness upon our lives.

—*Alfred A. Montapert*

★ ★ ★

ACHIEVEMENT

In his last baccalaureate sermon delivered at
Antioch College, Horace Mann admonished:
*"And I beseech you to treasure up in your hearts these my
parting words: Be ashamed to die till you have won some
victory for humanity."*

★ ★ ★

IMAGINATION

Imagination ... what magic power you possess!

—*Alphonse Daudet*

★ ★ ★

YOUTH AND AGE

Young men for action....
They have the enthusiasm, the power.
Old men for counsel...
They have the experience, the know-how.

—*Alfred A. Montapert*

★ ★ ★

GLADNESS

Life can be beautiful for those who have eyes to see and ears to hear. For eyes that perceive the invisible, and ears that hear the music of the Spheres. God has given us life to be lived with enthusiasm and joy. He has placed everything under our feet, endowed us with heads to think and hearts to feel. It is all up to us to enjoy our journey.

—*Rabbi Magnin*

★ ★ ★

INSPIRATION

Esprit de corps ... Morale ... Heart.
They are all different words meaning
the same thing ... INSPIRED PEOPLE.

—*Carl C. Wood*

★ ★ ★

KISS

With a Kiss...
Let us set out
For an unknown world.

—*Musset*

WHAT IS PHILOSOPHY?

Everyone has a philosophy, and your philosophy is what YOU believe, YOUR thoughts, YOUR ideals, YOUR eternal pursuit of truth and wisdom. As we think, we live; and how we live may be a pretty good indication of how we think.

—*Supreme Philosophy of Man*

★ ★ ★

GOODNESS

In and by itself, BOOK LEARNING
is not enough for the attainment of
happiness and peace of mind.
The world is full of educated idiots.
Love, Goodness and Righteousness
exalteth a person, not intellect.

—*Alfred A. Montapert*

★ ★ ★

THIS, TOO, SHALL PASS AWAY

Since life is short,
    We need to make it broad;
Since life is brief,
    We need to make it bright;
Then keep the old King's motto well in sight,
    And let its meaning permeate each day
Whatever comes ... "This, too, shall pass away."

—*Ella Wheeler Wilcox*

★ ★ ★

AT EASE

True politeness is perfect ease and freedom; it simply consists in treating others just as you love to be treated yourself.

—*Lord Chesterfield*

PERFECTION

To ENHANCE the quality
of the day...
That is the highest
of arts.

—Thoreau

★ ★ ★

DREAMS

An hour of study a day,
And a will to see it through,
To plan, to work, to pray,
Will make your dreams come true.

—Charles "Tremendous" Jones

★ ★ ★

BROKEN DREAMS

How often our DREAMS are broken—
suddenly, unexpectedly, sorrowfully.

—Alfred A. Montapert

★ ★ ★

WORRY

WORRY is a misuse of the imagination.
It is assuming responsibility that God never intended you to
have. It brings sorrow and saps the day of its strength.

—Alfred A. Montapert

★ ★ ★

IMAGINATION

Disneyland ... will never be completed as long as there is
imagination left in the world.

*—Walt Disney
July 15, 1955*

PERSEVERE

When you get into a tight place and everything goes against you, till it seems as though you could not hold on a minute longer, never give up, for that is just the place and time that the tide will turn.

—*Harriet Beecher Stowe*

★ ★ ★

ENTHUSIASM

Enthusiasm without a worthy purpose is piffle.

—*Alfred A. Montapert*

★ ★ ★

I WOULD BE TRUE

I would be true, for there are those who trust me;
I would be pure, for there are those who care;
I would be strong, for there is much to suffer;
I would be brave, for there is much to dare;
I would be friend of all—the foe, the friendless;
I would be giving, and forget the gift;
I would be humble, for I know my weakness;
I would look up, and laugh, and love, and lift.

—*Howard Arnold Walter*

★ ★ ★

THANK YOU

No better words than "thank you" have yet been discovered to express the sincere gratitude of one's heart—when the two words are sincerely spoken.

—*Alfred A. Montapert*

★ ★ ★

THE BEST THINGS IN LIFE ARE FREE

Sunshine, songs of birds, the blue heavens, sunrise, the sea air, the field full of flowers, the magenta sunset, love, joy, peace of mind, the wonders of nature, the warm rain, the dew on the roses, the love of God, etc., are here for our enjoyment.

—Alfred A. Montapert

★ ★ ★

CHANGE

God grant me the serenity
to accept the things I cannot change,
the courage to change the things I can,
and the wisdom to know the difference.

—Reinhold Niebuhr

★ ★ ★

TEARS

For all the trials and tears of time,
For every hill I have to climb,
My heart sings but a grateful song...
These are the things that make me strong.

—Anon.

★ ★ ★

IMAGINATION

The opportunities of man are limited only by his imagination. But so few have imagination that there are ten thousand fiddlers to one composer.

—Charles F. Kettering

★ ★ ★

GROWTH

There is no royal road to anything.
One thing at a time, all things in succession.
That which grows fast, withers as rapidly.
That which grows slowly, endures.

—*Josiah Gilbert Holland*

* * *

IMAGINATION

Your imagination, your capacity to day-dream or fanta-size, to relive the past, or to travel into the "future" through your mind's eye, is one of the greatest resources you have as a human being.

—*Jerome L. Singer*

* * *

SOUL

To hear the whispered voice
Of another's heart,
And understand unspoken words,
Are talents of those lucky few
People who are precious to the world.

—*Theresa Ann Hunt*

* * *

POETRY

Whatever may be your occupation,
However crowded your hours,
Do not fail to refresh your
Inner life with some poetry.

—*Alfred A. Montapert*

* * *

JOY

JOY is not in things:
It is in US.

—*Wagner*

★ ★ ★

DREAMS

Man's dream is first of WEALTH—then of LOVE.

—*Charles "Tremendous" Jones*

★ ★ ★

LOVE IS ETERNAL

The man or woman you really love will never grow old to you. Through the wrinkles of time, through the bowed frame of years, you will always see the dear face and feel the warm heart union of your eternal love.

—*Alfred A. Montapert*

★ ★ ★

HAPPINESS

HAPPY is the person who possesses...
UNBOUNDED ENTHUSIASM FOR LIFE

—*Anon.*

★ ★ ★

KNOWLEDGE

Knowledge is worth more than riches.

—*Proverb*

★ ★ ★

HELP-MATE

Behind every successful man you will find a good woman. There is a woman at the beginning of all great things.

—*Personal Planning Manual*

DREAMS

In your wagers with the world—
Put your bets on dreams, not ideas.

—*William D. Montapert*

★ ★ ★

OBSERVATION AND EXPERIENCE

See everything...
Overlook a great deal.
Correct a little.

—*Pope John XXIII*

★ ★ ★

INSPIRATION

Let us, then, be up and doing,
With a heart for any fate;
Still achieving, still pursuing,
Learn to labour and to wait.

—*Longfellow*

★ ★ ★

SUCCESS

Life's prizes are not gifts ... they must be won. It is up to each one to earn his rightful place in the world through developed ability and hard work. When one gets to love his work, his life is a HAPPY one.

—*Alfred A. Montapert*

★ ★ ★

TODAY

Whatever be thy fate today,
Remember...
"This too will pass away!"

—*Anon.*

CHAPTER 2

MOTIVATION

Action . . . . . . Encouragement . . . . . . Drive . . . . . .
Opportunity . . . . Effort . . . . Creativity

MOTIVATION

MOVE OUT, MAN! LIFE IS FLEETING BY.
DO SOMETHING WORTHWHILE, BEFORE YOU DIE.
LEAVE BEHIND A WORK SUBLIME,
THAT WILL OUTLIVE YOU, AND TIME!

—*Alfred A. Montapert*

★ ★ ★

Always do right.
This will gratify some people
and astonish the rest.

—*Mark Twain*

★ ★ ★

EFFORT

EVERY DAY

YOU WRITE

YOUR OWN

PAYCHECK!

—*Alfred A. Montapert*

★ ★ ★

RIGHT MOTIVATION

It doesn't make any difference who says a thing, or what the position of the man may be. The great question is: Is he RIGHT, OR is he WRONG?

—*Bernard Baruch*

BE

A DOER...

NOT

A TALKER.
—*Alfred A. Montapert*

★ ★ ★

COURTESY

COURTESY IS THE QUALITY
THAT MOST EASILY LIFTS ONE ABOVE THE CROWD.
—*Alfred A. Montapert*

★ ★ ★

BE A DOER

It is not always what you THINK,
Or what you BELIEVE,
Or what you KNOW.
It is what YOU DO!
Put FEET on your prayers.
Pray for those in need ... BUT,
Also take them a bag of groceries.
—*Distilled Wisdom*

★ ★ ★

SELF-EXPRESSION

I quote others only the better
to express myself.
—*Michel de Montaigne*

★ ★ ★

ZEST

In bad times and good,
I have never lost my sense of humor
or my zest for life.
—*Walt Disney*

WHAT DO I CONTRIBUTE TO LIFE?

George Bernard Shaw offered this cure for the problem of the over-populated human society: "A proposal that every citizen should be required to appear at reasonable intervals before a properly qualified jury to justify his existence. If he could not justify it, his existence would be swiftly and efficiently terminated."

★ ★ ★

ENCOURAGE

No man is great in and of himself; he must touch the lives of other great beings who will inspire him, lift him, and push him forward.

—*Alfred A. Montapert*

★ ★ ★

HAPPY

He that is of a merry heart
has a continual feast.

—*Proverbs 15:15*

★ ★ ★

DECISIONS

Run everything through your own mill.
If you are wrong,
Be wrong with your own decisions...
Not someone else's.

—*Alfred A. Montapert*

★ ★ ★

If it is to be,
It is up to me.

—*Anon.*

TO SPEAK OR WRITE

People are waiting to FEEL you...
Not just HEAR you.
The message must come from the HEART,
And it must come with conviction!

—*Alfred A. Montapert*

★ ★ ★

MAN'S TWO CREATORS

MAN HAS TWO CREATORS:

His God ... and himself

The First Creator furnishes the raw material and other gifts.

The Second Creator is what WE make of ourselves. Each individual builds his own monument, or digs his own grave.

—*Alfred A. Montapert*

★ ★ ★

ENJOYMENT

On a garden wall in Peking, China, was a brass plate about two feet long with these words:

ENJOY YOURSELF.
IT IS LATER THAN YOU THINK!

Well, maybe it IS later than you think; why don't you do something about it?

—*Charles W. Miller*

★ ★ ★

TURNING POINT

The lowest ebb is the turn of the tide.

—*Henry Wadsworth Longfellow*

FORMULA

WISDOM is knowing what to do next.
SKILL is knowing how to do it.
VIRTUE is doing it.

—Anon.

★ ★ ★

RESULT

Before every action ask yourself...
Will this bring more monkeys on my back?
Will the result of my action
Be a Blessing or a Heavy Burden?

—Alfred A. Montapert

★ ★ ★

CAUTION

THINK before you LEAP!

—Pythagoras

★ ★ ★

ACTION

You cannot plow a field
by turning it over in your mind.
You have to get off your butt
and do something!

—Dail C. West

★ ★ ★

SELECT

Never send a boy
to do a man's job.

—Alfred A. Montapert

★ ★ ★

MOTIVES

Motives are invisible...
But they are the true test of character.

—Alfred A. Montapert

★ ★ ★

DESTINY

There is a destiny that makes us brothers;
None goes his way alone.
All that we send into the lives of others
Comes back into our own.

—Edwin Markham

★ ★ ★

HOPE

Hope keeps us going.
We hope for the discovery of some means of action that will
reduce our misfortunes, help us reach our goals, increase our
well-being.

—Alfred A. Montapert

★ ★ ★

ADVICE

Never give advice. Look at Socrates,
a noted Greek philosopher, who went around
giving good advice ... and they poisoned him.

—Anon.

★ ★ ★

FUTURE

When we look into the long avenue of the future and
see the good there is for each one of us to do, we realize, after
all, what a beautiful thing it is to work, and live, and to be
happy.

—Robert Louis Stevenson

NEW DAY

Each day is a new piece of road ... better ask God for directions. I pray that God will guide my every footstep and keep me in His path ... and may the words of my mouth and the meditations of my heart be in line with God's word.

—Alfred A. Montapert

★ ★ ★

TIME

Life is swift, the pace is great.
You will never HAVE time for anything.
If you need time to do things important,
You must MAKE the time.

—Personal Planning Manual

★ ★ ★

ADVENTURE

It isn't necessary to fly over the South Pole, climb the Matterhorn, nor swim the English Channel, to find adventure. Life itself is an adventure and a challenge. Selling goods or services is an adventure. Raising a family is an adventure. Running a business is an adventure. Doing things that lift or steer humanity to higher levels is not only an adventure but also a service to mankind and to God.

—Charles "Tremendous" Jones

★ ★ ★

THOUGHT

Every year of my life I grow more convinced that it is wisest and best to fix our attention on the beautiful and the good, and dwell as little as possible on the evil and the false.

—Richard Cecil

★ ★ ★

OPPORTUNITY

There is a tide in the affairs of men, which, taken at the flood, leads on to fortune; omitted, all the voyage of their life is bound in shallows and in miseries. On such a full sea are we now afloat, and we must take the current when it serves, or lose our ventures.

—*William Shakespeare*

★ ★ ★

TIME

Do you love LIFE?
Then do not squander TIME
for that is the stuff life is made of.

—*Sir Walter Scott*

★ ★ ★

THINK

What is the most important thing to do today?
Then do it NOW!

—*Alfred A. Montapert*

★ ★ ★

THIS PRESENT

How quickly will pass this PRESENT!
How soon each one of us shall have done with the things which we have and handle. How soon we shall be called to recognize the fullest extent of God's amazing provision for us. Until then ... help us to fulfill this calling of ours, to seek first to find the niche for which we were made and to occupy it completely.

—*Alfred A. Montapert*

★ ★ ★

LIFE'S FIRST LESSON

"AS A MAN THINKETH IN HIS HEART, SO IS HE."

A man should know all that can be known of the great power which he is using every day, by THINKING, ACTING, SPEAKING as he does. The first lesson to be learned in the School of Life, is to understand one's own personality or individuality, so as to estimate it at its true value; to be able to use it for good and to avoid using it for evil.

—Supreme Philosophy of Man

★ ★ ★

SELF-CONTROL

MAN IS MADE OR UNMADE BY HIMSELF.
FOR MAN TO CONQUER HIMSELF
IS THE FIRST AND NOBLEST VICTORY.
MAN CONTROLS HIS OWN PASSIONS,
EMOTIONS, FUTURE. WITHOUT SELF-CONTROL
THE GOOD LIFE IS IMPOSSIBLE.

—Alfred A. Montapert

★ ★ ★

FIRST CAUSES

Things do not just happen...
they come to pass by our thoughts,
actions and deeds;
both good and bad.

A person finds it hard to explain all the wonderful things that have happened to him during his lifetime.

—Alfred A. Montapert

★ ★ ★

THINK

"Men would rather die than THINK!"

—Anatole France

EFFORT

The heights by great men reached and kept
Were not attained by sudden flight,
But they, while their companions slept,
Were toiling upward in the night.

—Henry Wadsworth Longfellow

★ ★ ★

NOBLE DEEDS

Speak out in acts!
The time for words has passed,
And deeds alone suffice!

—Whittier

★ ★ ★

THE WINNER

Say—"Good morning" with your lips.
With your eyes, say—"I like you."
Have a happy, cheerful attitude.
These are the joys and fruits of Life.

—The Way to Happiness

★ ★ ★

TIME

The amount of TIME I have
is not as important
as what I do with it.

—Alfred A. Montapert

★ ★ ★

GOOD DEEDS

It is not only what we do,
but also what we do not do,
for which we are accountable.

—Moliere

CREATIVITY

Man has access to the entire mind of the Creator,
is himself the creator in the infinite.

—Emerson

★ ★ ★

ACTION

The joy of living comes from action, from
making the attempt, from the effort, not from
success.

—Sir Frances Chichester

★ ★ ★

PERFECTION

Men can alter their lives
By altering their attitudes.

—William James

★ ★ ★

THE PRESENT

This present lies so near us. It offers immediate rewards. It
urges us to "get ahead." It promises promotions. But whatever it can give us is only temporary ... except one thing: an
opportunity to invest with God in abiding things.

—Alfred A. Montapert

★ ★ ★

RETREAT

It is sometimes necessary to step backward
in order to go forward.

—French Saying

★ ★ ★

CREATIVITY

To read a beautiful poem now and then, to witness a good play, to see a fine picture occasionally, to hear good music, is refreshing and stimulating as nothing else in life is. And it is always a wonderful thing to be able to create and interpret, to write, to paint, to play, to sing, and to love.

—Alfred A. Montapert

★ ★ ★

DO THE IMPOSSIBLE

According to the theory of aerodynamics, as may be readily demonstrated through wind tunnel experiments, the bumblebee is unable to fly. This is because the size, weight and shape of his body in relation to the total wing-spread makes flying impossible. The bumblebee, being ignorant of these scientific truths, goes ahead and flies anyway and makes a little honey each day.

—Anon.

★ ★ ★

ACTION AND REACTION

"I truly believe that whatever you send into the lives of others, comes back into your own."

—Mary Kay Ash

★ ★ ★

FRIGHTEN

A good scare is worth more to a man
than good advice.

—E. W. Howe

★ ★ ★

RESPONSIBILITY

Assets make things possible, but people make them happen. Everything depends on people. Give people a FUNCTION and a RESPONSIBILITY, then hold them accountable and you will be surprised with the results you will get.

—Alfred A. Montapert

* * *

DO

Do what is do-able, rather than dream.

—Carl C. Wood

* * *

GETTING RESULTS

THINK BIG—
attempt great things;
BELIEVE BIG—
and you'll get BIG results.

—Anthony B. Montapert

* * *

TOO LATE

"Too late I grasp my shield after my wounds."

—Ovid

* * *

ACTION

Our nature lies in movement.
Absolute rest is death.

—Blaise Pascal

* * *

BLESSING

May the Light of Heaven
Shine through each day,
To warm your life,
and show the Way.

—*The Way to Happiness*

★ ★ ★

SMILES

The wise doctor will mix smiles with his every prescription, be it drugs, or words of advice. Real "smiley" smiles are among the great result-bringing essentials of success.

—*Abbott*

★ ★ ★

AN OLD TRUTH

The wheel that squeaks the loudest
Is the one that gets the grease.

—*Anon.*

★ ★ ★

ACT

A beefsteak in the ice box you possess, but it is of no value until it is eaten and becomes part of you. Only then will it do you good. A million-dollar idea is sterile until you put it to use.

—*Alfred A. Montapert*

★ ★ ★

MOTIVATION

We need to be motivated by a new Spirit from within. Stir us out of our apathy and put the fire of love and goodness in us to move and motivate us to bigger and better days.

—*Supreme Philosophy of Man*

CHAPTER 3

HAPPINESS

Joy ..... *Contentment* ..... *Beauty* ..... *Choice*

HAPPINESS

The Eternal Quest of Mankind Depends Upon...
THE CHARACTER OF YOUR THOUGHTS,
SOME VOCATION WHICH SATISFIES THE SOUL,
THE ABILITY TO GIVE VALUE TO YOUR
EXISTENCE.
FOR HAPPINESS DEPENDS UPON WHAT LIES
BETWEEN
THE SOLES OF YOUR FEET
AND THE CROWN OF YOUR HEAD.

—Alfred A. Montapert

★ ★ ★

THE WAY TO HAPPINESS

Keep your heart free from hate,
Your mind from worry.
Live simply. Expect little
Give much.

—Anon.

★ ★ ★

Most people are
about as happy as they
make up their minds to be.

—Abraham Lincoln

★ ★ ★

A PROGRAM FOR HAPPINESS

To live content with small means;

To seek elegance rather than luxury,
and refinement rather than fashion;

To be worthy, not respectable,
and wealthy, not rich;

To study hard, think quietly,
talk gently, act frankly;

To listen to the stars and birds,
to babes and sages with open heart;

To bear all cheerfully, do all bravely,
await occasions, hurry never;

In a word, to let the spiritual, unbidden and
unconscious, grow up through the common.

—*William Henry Channing*

★ ★ ★

BEAUTY

The earth is all enchanted ground.
Look upon yon bush, flaming with roses; listen, if
thy soul be not deaf, thou wilt hear the voice of
God speaking to thee out of that bush.

—*Persian Saying*

★ ★ ★

WONDERFUL LIFE

MAKE UP YOUR MIND TO BE HAPPY. Learn to find
happiness in simple things. When the famous French writer,
Colette, was dying of cancer and was being interviewed by a
newsman, she exclaimed, *"What a wonderful life I've had! Those
were the happiest days!"* Then after a sigh of remorse, she
added, *"I only wish I'd realized it sooner."*

★ ★ ★

LAUGH

Always laugh when you can.
It is a cheap medicine.
Laughter is a tonic for your health.
It calms stress, fear, tempers, and
relieves the great strain of modern life.

—*Persis Hoeschen*

* * *

LOVE

We will always be together,
Now and for all time to be.
And I'll love you forever...
Beyond eternity.
I'm happy when you're with me,
I'm blue when we're apart.
Without you it's just as
Tho I live without a heart.
However tough the journey,
You shorten every mile
By giving me encouragement
With your tender smile.
Beside you is to be beside
An Angel from above.
I live and breathe for you alone;
You are my love.
I live to make you happy,
On that you can rely,
Always and always darling,
Until the day I die.
I hope you now know, dearest,
Just how much I care.
Life would be a dark abyss
Without your love to share.

—*Ben Burroughs*

* * *

HAPPINESS

There is only one person in the world who can really make you happy ... and YOU are that person. Happiness is a do-it-yourself job.

—Alfred A. Montapert

★ ★ ★

A PRACTICAL QUESTION

The question that faces every man born into this world is not what should be his purpose, or what he should set about to achieve, but just what to do with life. A life which is given him for a period of, on the average, fifty or sixty years. The answer that he should order his life so that he can find the greatest happiness in it is more a practical question, similar to that of how a man should spend his week-end, than a metaphysical proposition as to what is the mystic purpose of his life in the scheme of the universe.

—Lin Yutang

★ ★ ★

BE HAPPY

Laugh a lot.
Don't take yourself
Or your money
Too seriously!

—Dwight D. Eisenhower

★ ★ ★

WANTS

Contentment consists not in great wealth,
but in few wants.

—Epictetus

★ ★ ★

COMMITMENT

To achieve peace of mind,
most people need a commitment to work
in the service of some cause
they can respect.
Joy comes only from what we have done
to earn it.

—Dr. Hans Selye

* * *

CHOICES

We make choices and our choices determine how we come out. Whatsoever WE SOW, WE REAP. The law is— LIKE produces LIKE. Plant corn and you harvest corn, not tomatoes.

—Alfred A. Montapert

* * *

JOY

The chief product of life is really JOY!
JOY makes the face shine and is contentment
that fills the soul.

—Alfred A. Montapert

* * *

BEAUTY

We love beauty at first sight, but we do cease to love it if it is not accompanied by amiable qualities.

—Lydia Maria Child

* * *

THE INDWELLING PRESENCE

Always strive to have
a state of inward happiness,
independent from circumstances.
The indwelling Presence of God
will bring about this condition.

—*Alfred A. Montapert*

★ ★ ★

ATTITUDE

There is only one way to be happy,
and that is to make somebody else so.

—*Sidney Smith*

★ ★ ★

JOY

Let us celebrate
The occasion
With wine
and sweet words.

—*Lover*

★ ★ ★

PURE ENJOYMENT

The one who does not get fun and enjoyment out of every day in which he lives needs to reorganize his life. And the sooner the better. For pure enjoyment through life has more to do with one's happiness and efficiency than almost any other single element.

—*George Matthew Adams*

★ ★ ★

SPECIAL FRIENDS

The animals of the earth are among God's special creatures. They help us to work, carry us, guard our homes, and best of all, they bring us joy and laughter.

—*St. Francis of Assisi*

PLEASURE

You can't live on amusement.
It is the froth on water, an inch deep,
and then the mud!

—*George Macdonald*

★ ★ ★

LAUGH

A good laugh is sometimes better than medicine.

—*Anthony B. Mcntapert*

★ ★ ★

WHAT WE ARE

Happiness and contentment are not commodities which we import; neither do they depend upon "the abundance of things" which we possess. It is not where we are, what we have, or what we possess that makes us happy or unhappy. WHAT WE ARE determines our state. A very poor man can be immensely wealthy and a very rich man can be abjectly miserable. The most blessed kind of happiness is a state of basic contentment. St. Paul said, "*In whatever state I find myself, I have learned to be content.*"

—*Alfred A. Montapert*

★ ★ ★

HAPPY

Always keep that happy attitude.
Pretend that you are holding a beautiful fragrant bouquet.

—*Candice M. Pope*

★ ★ ★

YOUTH

I am not young enough to know everything.

—*James M. Barrie*

CONTENTMENT

The joys of life...
Porridge and soup,
A donkey to ride,
And a wife to drive it.

—Arab Proverb

★ ★ ★

RICHES WITH CONTENTMENT

Who is rich?
He who rejoices in his portion.

—Anon.

★ ★ ★

CITY

How good it is to see again
The skyline of one's own city.

—Alfred A. Montapert

★ ★ ★

LAUGHTER

Laugh and the world
laugh with you.
Cry and you weep alone.

—Ella Wheeler Wilcox

★ ★ ★

SATISFACTION

There are two things to aim at in life:
First, to get what you want;
And after that, to enjoy it.
Only the wisest of mankind achieve the second.

—Logan Pearsall Smith

WORTHWHILE LIVING

As long as you are close to me
I'll conquer every fear,
And do my best to bring you joy
And make you happy, dear.
So long as you give me your love
My heart will shed life's rain,
And I will weather every storm
Till sunlight shines again.
You give me the strength I need
To do the things I must,
And so it is I'll need your love
Until I turn to dust.
Because without your tenderness
My life would cease to be,
And I would drift about the world
Alone and all at sea.
So shower me with kisses, dear,
And cause my heart to smile,
For you, you alone, my love,
Make living so worthwhile.

—*Een Burroughs*

* * *

KINDNESS

A tiny bouquet of fresh-cut flowers,
Can fill a room with sunshine.
A little act of kindness
Can fill a heart with joy.

—*Katherine Nelson*

* * *

BLESSING

THE BLESSING OF THE LORD
IT MAKETH RICH...
AND ADDETH NO SORROW THEREWITH.

—*Evelyn W. Montapert*

BEING HAPPY

A marvelous thought came to me one day that is priceless, and I use it daily. I realized that I had the tremendous power to choose—so why not be happy? It's just as easy to choose to be happy as to be unhappy.

I have available to me the love and help of the HIGHEST POWER (GOD), who maintains the functions of the entire Universe. So I make myself available to this Power and this Unseen Force helps me with my writing. Helps me in everything I do. Helps me to be happy. This Supreme Power is the best thing I have going for me in my life.

—*Alfred A. Montapert*

★ ★ ★

CONTENTMENT

The secret of contentment
is knowing how to enjoy what you have,
and to be able to lose
all things beyond your reach.

—*Lin Yutang*

★ ★ ★

BALANCE

Enjoy what you can and endure what you must.

—*Goethe*

★ ★ ★

JOY

JOY is the flag
On the castle of your heart,
When the King is in residence.

—*Anon.*

★ ★ ★

THE GOLDEN RULE

"Whatsoever ye would that men should do to you, do ye even so to them." (Matthew 7:12)

Whenever a man analyzes his life, he finds that all of his happiness comes from doing good and loving others; and that all of his unhappiness comes from selfishness and hate.

—*Alfred A. Montapert*

★ ★ ★

LAUGHTER

Laughter is good to see
On a girl with white teeth.

—*Anon.*

★ ★ ★

PRESENCE

Some people
Make the world brighter
Just by being in it.

—*Mary Dawson Hughes*

★ ★ ★

BEAUTY

One should derive the keenest delight from scenery, trees and foliage, fruit and flowers, the blue sky, the fleecy clouds, the sparkling sea, the ripple on the lake, the gleam on the river, the shadows on the grass, the moon and stars at night.

—*John Lubbock*

★ ★ ★

HAPPINESS

Happiness is owning a stock
That doubles in a year.

—Charles "Tremendous" Jones

★ ★ ★

ENJOY NOW!

People spend their lives in anticipation of being extremely happy in the future. But all we own is the PRESENT ... NOW.

PAST opportunities are gone. FUTURE opportunities may, or may not, come. NOW is all we have.

We must enjoy each day—one at a time. We are here on a short visit. Be sure to smell the flowers.

—Alfred A. Montapert

★ ★ ★

BEAUTY

Could there be anything more beautiful than the early dawn, when the sun, just before it appears over the horizon, throws glorious colors into the sky; or when again, in the evening, the setting sun leaves its light reflected in hues against the clouds in the heavens?

—William C. Ross

★ ★ ★

HAPPY CHOICE

ARE YOU SPENDING YOUR LIFE DOING THE THINGS THAT GIVE YOU THE GREATEST HAPPINESS? YOU ONLY HAVE ONE LIFE TO LIVE, SO YOU MAY AS WELL DO SOMETHING THAT MAKES YOU HAPPY.

—Supreme Philosophy of Man

★ ★ ★

CHAPTER 4

SELF-DEVELOPMENT

Ability . . . . Emotion . . . . Self-Discovery.
Discipline . . . . Kindness . . . . Education.
Books . . . . . Pride . . . . . Learning . . . . . Pain . . . . .

PROBLEMS

The man who has
no more problems to solve,
is out of the game.

—Elbert Hubbard

★ ★ ★

ABILITY

The severest test of a businessman's ACUMEN and ABILITY
sometimes lies in the SPEED and MANNER with which he
RECOGNIZES, and GRASPS, the OPPORTUNITIES presented by the vagaries of fate.

—J. Paul Getty

★ ★ ★

SELF-CONTROL

He who reigns within HIMSELF,
and rules PASSIONS,
DESIRES and FEARS,
is more than a KING.

—Milton

★ ★ ★

EARNESTNESS

Earnestness is the QUALITY that convinces others.

In the last analysis, earnestness born of deep, clear, intelligent conviction...

>...is a fire that burns
>...a hammer that breaks
>...a sword that pierces.

It becomes the contagious enthusiasm which persuades and moves men to ACT.

The world is waiting not so much to hear us as to feel us.

Only hearts can speak to hearts.

And it is the language of the heart for which men are listening.

We can make others FEEL only what we FEEL.

—Alfred A. Montapert

★ ★ ★

BALANCE

There is nothing STABLE in human affairs
...therefore...
avoid undue elation in PROSPERITY
or undue depression in ADVERSITY
and don't let the bastards grind you down.

—Distilled Wisdom

★ ★ ★

WILL POWER

Your WILL is a tremendously important thing. We need to DEVELOP a strong WILL to help us make the proper CHOICES, just as we DEVELOPED our muscles from the time we were infants. A strong WILL builds ENERGY, HAPPINESS, CHARACTER and GOODNESS.

—Alfred A. Montapert

★ ★ ★

PROGRESS

BEHOLD THE TURTLE...
He makes progress only
        when he sticks his neck out.

—James Bryant Conant

★ ★ ★

EXPERIENCE

You don't LEARN HOW to swim
on paper.
You have to get into the water!

—Evelyn W. Montapert

★ ★ ★

HOLD STEADY

Don't take off your shoes
until you get to the creek.

—Senator Carl Vinton

★ ★ ★

KINDNESS

Getting money is not all a man's business; to cultivate kindness is a valuable part of the business of life.

—Dr. Samuel Johnson

ENJOY LIFE

Ask yourself:
1. Am I doing the things that make me happy?
2. Are my thoughts of noble character?
3. How can I simplify my life?
4. What are my talents?
5. Does my work satisfy my soul?
6. Am I giving value to my existence?
7. How can I improve my way of life?

—Alfred A. Montapert

★ ★ ★

DISCIPLINE

For years we have listened to some quack theorists and pseudo-psychologists who have preached that discipline and control were bad for children—that they should be left uninhibited to work out their own life patterns, their own self-discipline. But you don't acquire self-discipline if you never learn what discipline is.

Now we are reaping the harvest.

—J. Edgar Hoover

★ ★ ★

ENJOYMENT

Enjoy the little you have...
While the fool is hunting for more.

—Spanish Proverb

★ ★ ★

FISHMARKET TALK

The louder he talked of his honor,
the faster we counted our spoons.

—Ralph Waldo Emerson

★ ★ ★

THE OPTIMIST CREED

Promise Yourself—

To be so strong that nothing can disturb your peace of mind.

To talk health, happiness and prosperity to every person you meet.

To make all your friends feel that there is something in them.

To look at the sunny side of everything and make your optimism come true.

To think only of the best, to work only for the best, and to expect only the best.

To be just as enthusiastic about the success of others as you are about your own.

To forget the mistakes of the past and press on to the greater achievements of the future.

To wear a cheerful countenance at all times and give every living creature you meet a smile.

To give so much time to the improvement of yourself that you have no time to criticize others.

To be too large for worry, too noble for anger, too strong for fear, and too happy to permit the presence of trouble.

—*Optimist International*

★ ★ ★

SELF-DEVELOPMENT

Unfortunately, governments cannot legislate decency or integrity or goodness. Each individual must develop this power within himself. Man is raw and wild. We overlook the natural fact that we are here primarily to overcome the weakness of our own character.

—*Alfred A. Montapert*

★ ★ ★

MODERATION

MODERATION is one of the most
important words in the dictionary
and to practice in your lifetime.
NOT TOO MUCH ... NOT TOO LITTLE
and avoid all EXTREMES.

—*Alfred A. Montapert*

★ ★ ★

BOOKS

Some good book is usually responsible for the success of every really great man. By its counsel a book teaches a person how to live.

—*Charles "Tremendous" Jones*

★ ★ ★

BREVITY

Let thy speech be short, comprehending much in few words.

—*Ecclesiastes*

★ ★ ★

DOER

I like a person who bites off
more than he can chew, then chews it.

—*A. P. Gouthey*

GOOD WILL

The most precious thing anyone—man or store, any-body or anything—can have is the good will of others. It is something as fragile as an orchid. And as beautiful! As precious as a gold nugget—and as hard to find. As powerful as a great turbine, and as hard to build. As wonderful as youth—and as hard to keep.

—Amos Parrish

★ ★ ★

TRUE EDUCATION

Every individual has THREE DIVINE DIMENSIONS—
BODY ... MIND ... and SPIRIT.
Education which does not include the WHOLE PERSON
is NOT TRUE EDUCATION.

—Alfred A. Montapert

★ ★ ★

IN VAIN WE BUILD

We are blind until we see,
That in the human plan,
Nothing is worth the making if
It does not make the man.
Why build these cities glorious
If man unbuilded goes?
In vain we build the world, unless
The builder also grows.

—Edwin Markham

★ ★ ★

KINDNESS

It is a little embarrassing that after forty-five years of research and study, the best advice I can give to people is to be a little kinder to each other.

—Aldous Huxley

ROTARY CREED:

THE FOUR-WAY TEST
of the things we think, say or do.
First...
Is it the TRUTH?
Second...
Is it FAIR to all concerned?
Third...
Will it build GOODWILL and
BETTER FRIENDSHIP?
Fourth...
Will it be BENEFICIAL to all
concerned?

—*Rotary International*

* * *

SIMPLIFY

Simplicity of Life, simplicity of Faith ... Confidence, Hope,
Prayer, Trust, Things—all lose much of their value when they
lose their simplicity. The multiplicity of words and phrases
creates babble.

Simplify your life!

—*Richard W. Sampson*

* * *

CONVICTION

This man will go far,
for he believes
every word he says.

—*Mirabeau of Robespierre*

* * *

PRACTICAL EDUCATION

The purpose of education
is to learn something
you can use in the FUTURE.
When one acquires knowledge
BUT does not PRACTICE it,
it is like the fool
who plows the field
BUT does not plant it.

—Alfred A. Montapert

★ ★ ★

ANGER

Anger blows out the lamp of the mind. In
the examination of a great and important
question, everyone should be serene, slow-
pulsed and calm.

—Robert G. Ingersoll

★ ★ ★

THE BUILDER

Every MAN
is the Builder
of a Temple ...
called his BODY.

—Thoreau

★ ★ ★

ADVERSITY

A gem is not polished without friction,
nor a man perfected without trials.

—Anon.

★ ★ ★

EVERY PERSON IS UNIQUE

Every individual is a distinct unit that has no exact duplicate in the universe. That is true. That's easily discovered by a careful study of NATURE. Scientists tell us there are no two fingerprints alike, no two personalities alike.

This is the only personality I have, and I am responsible to God and men to develop it. That means that failure in the task assigned to me will determine my usefulness or lack of usefulness to God.

Each individual must FAIL or SUCCEED strictly on his own and there is no one else finally involved.

—*Charles "Tremendous" Jones*

★ ★ ★

YOUR DUTY

Your talents, skills, spirit, faculties ...
are God's bundle of GIFTS to you.
What you MAKE of yourself,
plus your service,
is YOUR GIFT to man and GOD.
You serve God by serving your fellowman.

—*Alfred A. Montapert*

★ ★ ★

LEARN

"All men make mistakes
but only wise men LEARN from their mistakes."

—*Winston Churchill*

★ ★ ★

LEARN

When you're through improving yourself
You're out of the game.
You learn until your last breath.

—*Richard A. Nelson*

★ ★ ★

ASK YOURSELF

What have I learned wherever I've been,
From all I've heard, from all I've seen?
What know I more that's worth the knowing?
What have I done that's worth the doing?
What have I sought that I should shun?
What duties have I left undone?

—*Pythagoras*

★ ★ ★

SELF-CONQUEST

You can conquer yourself to a degree
but not fully.
Total conquest is only made possible
by surrendering to God...
That is Christianity.

—*Alfred A. Montapert*

★ ★ ★

ENTHUSIASM

Enthusiasm is the mother of effort, and without it nothing great was ever accomplished. The successful person has enthusiasm. Every great achievement is the story of a flaming heart.

—*Emerson*

★ ★ ★

SENSES

Your SENSES will take you farther
than your intellect.

—*A. P. Gouthey*

* * *

ANGER

Arrows pierce the body,
But harsh words pierce the soul.

—*Spanish Proverb*

* * *

AWARENESS

How many opportunities are obscure
but available to a man
without his perceiving them?

—*Alfred A. Montapert*

* * *

BE READY

The secret of success in life
is for man to be ready
for his opportunity...
when it comes.

—*Disraeli*

* * *

LEGACY

All the great thoughts of all the great thinkers are yours to use and build upon.

Today, this very minute, you are heir to more accumulated wisdom, knowledge, and experience than man has ever before possessed. You could be a giant, if you knew and could apply this wisdom.

—*Fred Corbett*

KNOW THYSELF

When Thales was asked...
"What was difficult?" he said,
"To know one's self."
And what was easy?
"To advise another."

—*Diogenes Laertius*

★ ★ ★

DEVELOPMENT

The end of man is the highest
and most harmonious development
of his powers to a complete and
consistent whole.

—*W. Von Humboldt*

★ ★ ★

YOUR POTENTIAL

"If they can make penicillin out of
moldy bread, they can sure make
something out of you."

—*Muhammad Ali*

★ ★ ★

CRITICISM

It is much easier to be critical
than to be correct.

—*Disraeli*

★ ★ ★

NATURAL LAWS

As we learn to distill the salt of wisdom from the vast
ocean of man's experience, I believe we will discover patterns
that are clues to the natural laws governing human affairs.

—*Bernard Baruch*

BELIEF and FAITH

Man is what he believes.
For belief is the great force of the mind.
To accomplish great things, we must
DREAM ... PLAN ... ACT ... BELIEVE!

FAITH is your trust in the Mighty Power of God.
It is the fire in the heart.
Without it you are nothing!

FAITH and BELIEF—the unbeatable combination—
Make for LIFE ... HEALTH ... WEALTH ... and
HAPPINESS.

—*Alfred A. Montapert*

★ ★ ★

ANGER

Control your anger until you know the facts.
Anger clouds the soul,
And impedes your judgment.

—*Latin*

★ ★ ★

ADVICE

Nobody can give you
wiser advice
than yourself.

—*Cicero*

★ ★ ★

DISCRETION

I have never been hurt
by anything I didn't say.

—*Calvin Coolidge*

★ ★ ★

CHRISTIAN LIVING

When it comes to correcting and developing LIFE, it is purely a personal business between God and the individual. "Work out YOUR OWN SALVATION with fear and trembling" ... NOT work out someone else's.

—*Alfred. A. Montapert*

★ ★ ★

13th COMMANDMENT

Thou shalt mind thine own business.
I will, henceforth, concentrate on me,
and keep my nose out of others' business.

—*Alfred A. Montapert*

★ ★ ★

EXAMPLE

Rules make the learner's path long;
examples make it short and successful.

—*Seneca*

★ ★ ★

MODERATION

MODERATION IN ALL THINGS IS EXCELLENT.

—*Pythagoras*

★ ★ ★

STEADFAST

The secret of success
is constancy of purpose.

—*Disraeli*

★ ★ ★

GENTLEMAN

A GENTLEMAN IS HARDER TO FIND
THAN A GENIUS.

—Alfred A. Montapert

★ ★ ★

BEST GOVERNMENT

What government is best?
That which teaches us
to govern ourselves.

—Goethe

★ ★ ★

GOALS

What do you really want?
What are your goals?
When you honestly know,
Write it down and ACT upon it.
Only then do you automatically
have a personal goal,
And have given direction to your life.

—Personal Planning Manual

★ ★ ★

THE WILL

It's the action of THE WILL
that determines the conduct.

—William James

★ ★ ★

FUTURE

My interest is in the future...
because I am going to spend the rest of my life there.
That is my reason for planning.

—Charles F. Kettering

PRESS ON

Nothing in the world can take the place of
PERSISTENCE.
TALENT will not: nothing is more common than
unsuccessful men with talent.
GENIUS will not: unrewarded genius is almost
a proverb.
EDUCATION alone will not: the world is full
of educated derelicts.

PERSISTENCE AND DETERMINATION
alone are omnipotent.

—Calvin Coolidge

★ ★ ★

SILENCE

"To speak is to dilute one's thoughts, to give vent to one's
ardor; in short, to dissipate one's strength; whereas, what
action demands is concentration. Silence is a necessary
preliminary to the ordering of one's thoughts."

—General de Gaulle

★ ★ ★

TIMING

Timing is the chief ingredient
in judgment.

—William Feather

★ ★ ★

SEEKING

No man really becomes a fool
until he stops asking questions.

—Charles P. Steinmetz

★ ★ ★

EXTREME CALMNESS

No quality ranks with IMPERTURBABILITY. It is the essential bodily virtue.

IMPERTURBABILITY means coolness and presence of mind under all circumstances ... calmness amid storm ... clearness of judgment in moments of grave peril.

IMPERTURBABILITY is a blessing to you and a comfort to all who come in contact with you. With practice and experience you may expect to attain a fair measure.

The FIRST ESSENTIAL is extreme calmness, never to show or express anxiety or fear.

—Sir William Osler

★ ★ ★

CONCENTRATION

The power of concentration is one of the most valuable attainments in the management of human affairs. Keep the subject constantly in your mind, and hold it there until the first inkling opens slowly, little by little, into a full clear light.

—Richard A. Nelson

★ ★ ★

REALIZE

GUILT PRODUCES FEAR AND WORRY!
You'd better believe it.

—Alfred A. Montapert

★ ★ ★

TRAINING

The best training any parent can give a child is to train the child to train himself.

—*A. P. Gouthey*

* * *

PERSONAL RESPONSIBILITY

To Develop Ourselves
Is Life's Greatest
And Noblest Project...
Required of Each of Us!

—*Alfred A. Montapert*

* * *

BOOKS

A great library contains the diary
of the human race.

—*Dawson*

* * *

READING

Reading provides material with which to think, and thinking is an important factor in successful living. Those who will take pains to think things through and elaborate their ideas are likely to win out over the undisciplined efforts of other, perhaps brighter, people.

—*Alfred A. Montapert*

* * *

OBLIGING

We cannot always oblige,
but we can always speak obligingly.

—*Voltaire*

SCHOOL

School is but a mental gymnasium. The best thing a school can teach you is how to THINK for yourself. LOGICAL THINKING AND GOOD LISTENING should become a way of life. IF YOU ARE NOT LISTENING, YOU ARE NOT LEARNING. John Lubbock writes, *"Reading and writing, arithmetic, and grammar, do not constitute education, any more than a knife, fork, and spoon, constitute a dinner."*

—*Alfred A. Montapert*

★ ★ ★

PREPARE

I'll study and get ready and then maybe my chance will come.

—*Lincoln*

★ ★ ★

BOOKS

Many useful and valuable books lie buried in shops and libraries unknown and unexamined, unless some lucky compiler opens them by chance and finds an easy spoil of wit and learning.

—*Samuel Johnson*

★ ★ ★

DISCIPLINE

The greatest need of the United States is DISCIPLINE and PRIDE. The greatest need of any individual is SPIRITUAL DEVELOPMENT—oneness with God, the HIGHER POWER.

—*Alfred A. Montapert*

★ ★ ★

GREATNESS

There is a kind of greatness which does not depend upon fortune; it is a certain manner that distinguishes us, and which seems to destine us for great things; it is the value we insensibly set upon ourselves; it is by this quality that we gain the deference of other men, and it is this which commonly raises us more above them than birth, rank, or even merit itself.

—*Francois de La Rochefoucauld*

★ ★ ★

ALONE

Every man must do two things alone—
he must do his own believing
and his own dying.

—*Martin Luther*

★ ★ ★

RELY ON YOURSELF

In battle or business,
whatever the game,
In law, or in love,
it is ever the same;
In the struggle for power,
or the scramble for pelf
Let this be your motto—
"Rely on yourself."

—*J. G. Saxe*

★ ★ ★

GOODNESS

Goodness is the only investment that never fails.

—*Henry David Thoreau*

★ ★ ★

EDUCATION

Every man has two educations: one which he receives from others; and one, more important, which he gives himself.

—Gibbon

* * *

SELF-DISCIPLINE

The most valuable of all education is the ability to make yourself do the thing you have to do when it has to be done, whether you like it or not.

—Aldous Huxley

* * *

KNOW YOURSELF

"Know yourself" is still good advice. Determine not only what your likes are but where are your special abilities. Choose the field in which you will be happiest, and the track on which you can go farthest, not necessarily fastest.

—Alfred A. Montapert

* * *

STUDY

If you do not want to commit suicide, always have something to do. A long life has time to combat time. Books rule the world. Nothing enfranchises like education. When once a nation begins to think, it is impossible to stop it.

—Voltaire

* * *

SELF-CONTROL

It takes a little courage
    And a little self-control
And some grim determination,
    If you want to reach the goal.

It takes a deal of striving,
    And a firm and stern-set chin,
No matter what the battle,
    If you really want to win.

There's no easy path to glory,
    There's no rosy road to fame.
Life, however we may view it,
    Is no simple parlor game;

But its prizes call for fighting,
    For endurance and for grit;
For a rugged disposition
    And a don't-know-when-to-quit.

—Anon.

★ ★ ★

OUR TASK

The whole of life...
    Is our individual task...
        To develop our full potential.
—Alfred A. Montapert

★ ★ ★

CONQUER SELF

The first and best victory is to conquer
    self; to be conquered by self is, of
        all things, most shameful and vile.
—Plato

★ ★ ★

LEARNING

Learning to learn is to know how to navigate in a forest of facts, ideas and theories. A proliferation of constantly changing items of knowledge.

Learning to learn is to know what to ignore but at the same time not rejecting innovation and research.

—Queneau

★ ★ ★

EDUCATION

The aim of education should be to teach the child to think, not WHAT to think.

—John Dewey

★ ★ ★

RECIPROCITY

By learning, you will teach;
By teaching, you will learn.

—Latin Proverb

★ ★ ★

GRADUATION

The final exams were only paper work for marks. The real test is now coming up. Now that you are on your own, it is "for keeps." Years of study in which you were led and nourished by teachers have readied you for the effort, but NOW the effort is all yours. NOW you move out into the arena where your survival depends upon learning the rest of the alphabet.

—Alfred A. Montapert

★ ★ ★

THE CLOCK OF LIFE

The clock of life is wound but once
    And no man has the power

To tell just when the hands will stop—
    At late or early hour.

NOW is the only time you own,
    LIVE, LOVE, TOIL with a will.

Place no faith in "tomorrow," for
    The clock may then be still.

—Unknown

★ ★ ★

READING

The man who is endeavoring to develop his judgment will profit by imitating an acquaintance of mine, who realizes that no individual's judgment can be any better than the information at his command.

He reads incessantly, books produced by the best minds in the country. AS HE FINISHES EACH CHAPTER, HE ANALYZES IT AND MAKES A CONDENSED DIGEST OF IT. He picks all of the meat out so that the substance can be read, perhaps, in a minute or less. When he finishes with each book, he has fifteen or twenty closely typed pages giving the contents of the book in all of the important essentials, even though it may have covered, in the original, fully two or three hundred pages. He covers a wide range of the subjects; changing conceptions of religion, philosophy, geography, biology and general news. Out of this, he has developed an amazing grasp of what men are doing and how they are thinking.

—Charles R. Gow

★ ★ ★

ENJOY

My theory is to enjoy life—
But the practice is against it.

—Lamb

★ ★ ★

PAIN

EVERYONE GETS KNOCKED DOWN,
BUT CHAMPIONS GET UP.

—Alfred A. Montapert

★ ★ ★

WAY OF LIFE

Nine people in ten are suicides…
Suicides by what they FAIL TO DO
and by what they OVER-DO.
Few people know how to live.
They kill themselves by their
"Way of Life."

—Alfred A. Montapert

★ ★ ★

GOOD-NATURED

When good-natured people leave us, we look forward
with extra pleasure to their return. I have a good friend who
has the ability to lift my burdens and brighten my day.

—Anita Hesselgesser

★ ★ ★

IDEA

There is nothing more powerful than an idea
whose time has come.

—Victor Hugo

CHAPTER 5

SUCCESSFUL LIVING

Success .... Growth .... Effort .... Leisure ....
Achievement..... Pleasure..... Enjoyment.....
Decisions .... Soul .... Time .... Conduct ....
Responsibility . .... Plan ...... Giving ......

ENJOY NOW

Live neither in the past nor in the future,
but let each day's work absorb all
your interest, energy, and enthusiasm. The
best preparation for tomorrow is to
do today's work superbly well.

—Sir William Osler

* * *

QUALIFICATIONS FOR SUCCESS

FIRST, is a big wastebasket.
You must know what to DISCARD.

SECOND, it is as important to know what to PRESERVE.

THIRD, do not offer, nor accept, unnecessary RESPONSIBILITIES.

FOURTH, learn HOW and WHEN to say NO, for developing the power to say NO gives us the capacity to say YES.

—Alfred A. Montapert

* * *

SUCCESS

To get PROFIT without RISK
...EXPERIENCE without DANGER
...and REWARD without WORK
...is as IMPOSSIBLE as it is
TO LIVE WITHOUT BEING BORN.

—Alfred A. Montapert

TEN RULES FOR SUCCESS

1. Find your own particular talent.
2. Be big.
3. Be honest.
4. Live with enthusiasm.
5. Don't let your possessions possess you.
6. Don't worry about your problems.
7. Look up to people when you can—down to no one.
8. Don't cling to the past.
9. Assume your full share of responsibility in the world.
10. Pray consistently and confidently.

—*Anon.*

★ ★ ★

SILENCE

There is no explanation quite so effective as silence. Explanations rarely explain. Those who demand explanations usually have their opinions formulated before you begin to explain. If you are right, your life will do its own explaining. If you are wrong, you can't explain. So, go calmly on your way and forget everything but the business of right living—and let time explain you.

—*Alfred A. Montapert*

★ ★ ★

SAFEGUARD

The greatest safeguard to this nation,
or any other nation, is the teaching
of THE WORD OF GOD. Real security
is having a SENSE OF GOD.
A person can no more build a life
without solid beliefs and ideals
than he can build a building
without a solid foundation.

—*Charles "Tremendous" Jones*

SUCCESSFUL LIVING

What good is our present progress through technology and science if we fail to become better people? The fact is, that EACH OF US IS RESPONSIBLE FOR WHAT WE MAKE OF OUR OWN LIFE. The Government cannot play God and create people who are identical in ability. This development is an INDIVIDUAL RESPONSIBILITY.

—Personal Planning Manual

* * *

EFFORT

When we have done our BEST—
we should await the result with great
expectations.
Then the important thing is to know how
to take all things QUIETLY.

—Alfred A. Montapert

* * *

LIFE

When I hear somebody sigh that
"Life is hard,"
I am always tempted to ask...
"Compared to what?"

—Sidney Harris

* * *

GOALS

If a person does NOT have any GOALS ... he is empty inside and ready to visit a psychiatrist, or driven to other pills.

—Richard A. Nelson

* * *

SUCCESSFUL MEN

Successful men usually snatch success
from seeming defeat.
If they know there is such a word as
failure, they will not admit it.
They may be whipped but they are not
aware of it ... THEY FIGHT ON.
THAT is WHY they SUCCEED!

—Alfred A. Montapert

★ ★ ★

SUCCESS

When you have both GOLD and GOODNESS,
you have reached
the high plateau of living.

—Supreme Philosophy of Man

★ ★ ★

BE BRIEF

Unless you are brief,
your complete plan of thought
will seldom be grasped.
Before you reach the conclusion,
the reader or listener has forgotten
the beginning and the middle.

—Horace

★ ★ ★

WHAT IS LIVING?

Life is a curious gift. It brings in its train both joy and
sorrow, pleasure and pain ... above all, experience, which
we can use or neglect to use. To live, in the fullest sense, is to
be in harmony with the higher power and live by the laws of
Nature.

—Evelyn W. Montapert

★ ★ ★

CONDUCT

May everything I say and do
be pleasing in God's sight.
God is greater than any problem
I have or ever will have.

"Rest in the Lord,"
put your trust in God,
and you begin to truly live.

—*Charles "Tremendous" Jones*

★ ★ ★

TIME

Every person will gravitate to his own level...
all it takes is time.
Time is the only sure test of anything.

—*Alfred A. Montapert*

★ ★ ★

ACHIEVE

There is no man living
who cannot do more
than he thinks he can.

—*Henry Ford*

★ ★ ★

FUTURE

I have but one lamp by which my feet are guided, and that is
the lamp of experience. I know of no way of judging the
future but by the past.

—*Patrick Henry*

★ ★ ★

TOIL

What I have done is due to past thought.

—*Newton*

VICTORIOUS LIVING

First make up your mind what you want to DO ... BE ...
HAVE.
Set your goals; establish your priorities.
Work out plans to reach those goals,
Then measure life and your days accordingly.

—*Alfred A. Montapert*

★ ★ ★

PLAN

He, who every morning plans the transactions of the day,
and follows out that plan, carries a thread that will guide him
through the labyrinth of the most busy life. The orderly
arrangement of his time is like a ray of light that darts itself
through all his occupations. But where no plan is laid, where
the disposal of time is surrendered merely to the chance of
accident, chaos will soon reign.

—*Victor Hugo*

★ ★ ★

YOU

To live his life to the most satisfying effect,
Every man must depend upon himself...
On his own thinking, on his own deciding,
And on his own doing...
On no one, and on nothing else.

—*Charles "Tremendous" Jones*

★ ★ ★

SELF-RESPECT

Without self-respect, there can be no genuine success.
Success won at the cost of self-respect is not success—for
what shall it profit a man if he gain the whole world and lose
his own self-respect?

—*B. C. Forbes*

SUCCESS

He has achieved success who has lived well, laughed often, and loved much; who has gained the respect of intelligent men and the love of little children; who has filled his niche and accomplished his task; who has left the world better than he found it, whether by an improved poppy, a perfect poem, or a redeemed soul; who has never lacked appreciation of earth's beauty, or failed to express it; who has always looked for the best in others and given the best he had; whose life was an inspiration; whose memory is a benediction.

—*Bessie A. Stanley*

* * *

MISSION FOR GOD

Now when I am old and grayheaded, O God,
forsake me not;
until I have shewed thy strength unto this generation,
and thy power to every one that is to come.

—*David; Psalm 71:18*

* * *

GIVE

You GIVE to get.
The surest way to get is to give—
and one's getting will be gauged by one's giving.
So said Christ.
So testifies experience.

—*Alfred A. Montapert*

* * *

SUCCESSFUL LIVING

THE MOST IMPORTANT THING TO LEARN IN LIFE IS...
"HOW TO LIVE."

That is the greatest question in life. I can live successfully and die without knowing plenty, but there are some basic truths that I must know to live successfully. I must fulfill the purpose for which I am here—and that purpose is to serve others.

—Alfred A. Montapert

★ ★ ★

POISE

Poise is a big factor in a man's success. If I were a young man just starting out, I would talk things over with myself as a friend. I would set out to develop poise—for it can be developed. A man should learn to stand, what to do with his hands, what to do with his feet, look another straight in the eye, dress well and look well, and know he locks well. By dressing well, I don't mean expensively, but neatly and in good taste.

—F. Edson White

★ ★ ★

THE PAST

The moving Finger writes;
And, having writ, moves on:
Nor all thy Piety nor Wit
Shall lure it back to cancel half a line,
Nor all thy Tears wash out a Word of it.

—Omar Khayyam

★ ★ ★

SIMPLICITY

Simplicity, Simplicity, Simplicity.

I say, let your affairs be as two or three, and not a hundred or a thousand; instead of a million, count half a dozen and keep your accounts on your thumbnail.

—Thoreau

★ ★ ★

TIME

So much to do.
So much to see.
Time is the enemy.

—Alfred A. Montapert

★ ★ ★

OTHERS

There would be little left of me
If I were to discard what
I owed to others.

—Goethe

★ ★ ★

ACHIEVE

"I have always believed that anybody with a little guts and the desire to apply himself can make it, can make anything he wants to make of himself—and that includes race riding."

—Willie Shoemaker
The World's Winningest Jockey

★ ★ ★

RESPONSIBILITY

All business depends upon men fulfilling their promises.

—Gandhi

ABILITY

"In my vocabulary, there is no such word as 'can't,'
because I recognize that my abilities
are given to me by God
to do what needs to be done."

—*Wofford B. Camp*

★ ★ ★

DAY

I have come to the conclusion
that you have to live every day,
do your best every day,
enjoy every day.
Each day is a little life.
Some days are better than others.

—*Alfred A. Montapert*

★ ★ ★

ESSENTIAL KNOWLEDGE

"I went to the woods," Thoreau wrote, "because I
wished to live deliberately, to confront only the essential
facts of life, and see if I could not learn what it had to teach;
and not, when I came to die, discover that I had not lived."

—*Thoreau*

★ ★ ★

TIME

The man who can master his time
can master nearly everything.

—*Bernard Baruch*

★ ★ ★

SILENCE

The older I grow, the more I see the value of silence. Pythagoras admonished, *"Be silent, or let thy words be worth more than silence."* The wisest retort is often silence. The words of a silent man are never brought to court.

—*Alfred A. Montapert*

★ ★ ★

SUCCESS

"My definition of success
is the achieving of the goals
one sets for one's self,
whatever they may be."

—*Michel T. Halbouty*

★ ★ ★

CHARACTER

Character is something each one of us must build for himself, out of the laws of God and Nature, the examples of others, and most of all—out of the trials and errors of daily life. Character is the total of thousands of small daily strivings to live up to the best that is in us.

—*Lt. General A. G. Trudeau*

★ ★ ★

EXPERIENCE

The more sand that has escaped
from the hourglass of our life,
the clearer we should see through it.

—*Jean Paul Richter*

★ ★ ★

SUNSHINE

There are some people who carry their wealth with them, who are rich without money. They do not need palatial homes or a large bank account. They do not need to buy admission to society—everybody loves them. They are welcome everywhere because they have that which money cannot buy—a genial, helpful, sunny, cheerful disposition.

—*Richard A. Nelson*

★ ★ ★

PRUDENCE

Men's lives are chains of chances...
But as Euripides admonished:
"Chance fights ever on the
side of the prudent."

—*Distilled Wisdom*

★ ★ ★

DECISION

"No" and "Yes" are words quickly said,
but they need a great amount of thought
before you utter them.

—*Baltasar Gracian*

★ ★ ★

ACCOMPLISHMENT

True success depends
More on character and goodness
Than on intellect.

—*Alfred A. Montapert*

★ ★ ★

CHANGE

As we look ahead, we recognize that life is never static but constantly changing. We must adapt ourselves to new conditions and new challenges as they arise. No person can live the abundant life without the help of the HIGHER POWER.

—*Alfred A. Montapert*

★ ★ ★

LONG LIFE

We have no right to look for a happy old age if, in our living, we habitually violate physical and spiritual laws. The full blessing of length of days comes to those who have known how to live, and the beauty of the years of maturity can be assured only by maintaining high standards of living.

—*Janet Baird*

★ ★ ★

STAY YOUNG

"The minute a man ceases to grow,
no matter what his years,
that minute he begins to be old."

—*William James*

★ ★ ★

TOO LATE

It is only when we have lost them,
That we fully appreciate our blessings.

—*Anon.*

★ ★ ★

LAW OF NATURE

Man lives in a world
Pervaded with Nature's laws
Just as a fish lives in water,
Or a bird lives in the air.

—Alfred A. Montapert

★ ★ ★

ANGER

ANGER WILL GET YOU NOWHERE.

—French Proverb

★ ★ ★

PURPOSE

WITHOUT A PURPOSE, NOTHING SHOULD BE DONE.

—Marcus Aurelius

★ ★ ★

DECISION

Best to sleep on it.
(Referring to making decisions.)

—French Proverb

★ ★ ★

DEBATE

When I'm getting ready to reason with a man, I spend one-third of my time thinking about myself and what I am going to say—and two-thirds thinking about him and what he is going to say.

—Abraham Lincoln

★ ★ ★

SOUL

"The destiny of man lies in his soul."

—Herodotus

CHARACTER

CHARACTER is a by-product. It is produced in the great manufacture of daily duty.

—Woodrow Wilson

* * *

REASON

A man always has two reasons
For doing anything...
A good reason—
And the real reason.

—J. P. Morgan

* * *

BUSINESS

Business will be either better or worse.

—Calvin Coolidge

* * *

GOOD DAY

It's a darn good day,
if you can put on your shoes
and go to work.

—Robert Burns

* * *

VIEWPOINT

Two men looked out through prison bars...
one saw mud;
the other stars.

—Anon.

* * *

TIMING

To everything there is a season,
And a time to every purpose
Under the heaven...
A time to be born,
And a time to die;
A time to plant,
And a time to pluck up
That which is planted.

—*King Solomon*

★ ★ ★

TIME

A friend of mine is very wise. He very deliberately estimates the time remaining to him and then acts accordingly. He checks to see that his affairs are in order. Writes to old friends he has long been intending to contact. Forgives people that he has been holding grudges against. Examines his relationship with God. Devotes more time to his loved ones—and then begins to spend a considerable amount of time looking back on the blessings he has experienced and looking forward to the adventure of eternity. He told me this has given him a remarkable feeling of serenity.

—*Alfred A. Montapert*

★ ★ ★

PLEASURE

Much pleasure and little grief
is every man's desire.

—*Spanish Proverb*

★ ★ ★

RIGHTS

I believe each individual is entitled
to do as he pleases with himself
and the fruits of his labor,
so far as it in no wise interferes
with any other man's rights

—Abraham Lincoln

★ ★ ★

FOOL

The shame lies not in having a fling,
But in not cutting it short.

—Horace

★ ★ ★

EXAMPLE

It is not enough to be an upright man;
we must be seen to be one.
Society does not exist on moral ideas only.

—Balzac

★ ★ ★

ILLUMINATE

One cool judgment is worth a dozen
hasty councils. The thing to do is
to supply LIGHT and not heat.

—Woodrow Wilson

★ ★ ★

TIME

Time is not measured by the passing of years but by what one
DOES ... what one FEELS ... and what one ACHIEVES.

—Nehru

LAW OF PROSPERITY

There is a Divine LAW of Prosperity,
by which we may avail ourselves
of the riches of God.

By getting in line with THE WORD OF GOD,
and confessing THE WORD with our mouth,
we can have unlimited supply
to meet all our needs.

The secret is ... we must learn to BELIEVE,
and be OBEDIENT to THE WORD,
and CONFESS THE WORD,

So that we make ourselves channels
of God's resources.

—*Alfred A. Montapert*

* * *

CONTRIBUTION

The ideal social state is not that
in which one gets an equal amount of
wealth, BUT in which each gets IN
PROPORTION TO HIS CONTRIBUTION TO
the general stock.

—*Henry George*

* * *

ENCOURAGEMENT

Illegitimi non carborundum.
(Don't let the bastards grind you down!)

—*Latin*

* * *

SELF-CONQUEST

Self-conquest is the greatest of all victories.

—*Plato*

SUCCESSFUL LIVING

The business of living is to build a LIFE, to make a good life. To make a living is secondary. The man we ought to be, shames the man that we are. We must fill our niche. We know that only we can fill it or it will not be filled.

—*Charles "Tremendous" Jones*

★ ★ ★

REAL WEALTH

Good health
A little common sense
A sense of God
A pleasant and confident attitude
A little love
A little good humor
A little cash

And you will be surprised how comfortable and contented you can be in a world where almost everyone is reaching for the moon.

—*Charles W. Miller*

★ ★ ★

DELIGHTFUL MELODIES

Music is good for the soul. The soothing melody of beautiful music can fill one's soul with satisfaction and joy. Nothing overcomes depression so easily and completely as a song, for the mind cannot brood while enjoying beautiful melodies.

—*Genevieve W. Sampson*

★ ★ ★

HOPE

Who could live without hope?

—*Carl Sandburg*

THE BEST

There is NO such thing
as highest and best living ...
ONLY as we come to
walk with God
on HIS high level.

—Alfred A . Montapert

★ ★ ★

CONVERSATION

One of the best rules in conversation
is never to say a thing which any of
the company can reasonably
wish had been left unsaid.

—Swift

★ ★ ★

CROWNING VIRTUE OF SILENCE

"Nothing more enhances authority than SI-
LENCE. It is the crowning virtue of the strong, the
refuge of the weak, the modesty of the proud, the
pride of the humble, the prudence of the wise."

—Charles De Gaulle

★ ★ ★

CAUTION

Let sleeping dogs lie.

—Greek Proverb

★ ★ ★

CONDUCT

Education is the ability to listen to almost anything without
losing your temper or your self-confidence.

—Robert Frost

DAILY CHORES

SUCCESS is like housekeeping—
    it's a daily chore.
You have to do it all over again
    every day.
You can't rest on your laurels.
Yesterday's hits won't win
    today's game.

—Anon.

★ ★ ★

RESULTS

Is this not what everything is all about?
Is this not what your goals are for?
Is this not what your life is all about?
The result proves the right way to live.
The result is the positive proof of the
    right solution and method.

—Alfred A. Montapert

★ ★ ★

LIFE

One of the most tragic things I know about human nature is that all of us tend to put off living. We are all dreaming of some magical rose garden over the horizon—instead of enjoying the roses that are blooming outside our windows today.

—Dale Carnegie

★ ★ ★

MUSIC

Music washes away from the soul
    the dust of everyday life.

—Berthold Auerbach

HUMAN VALUES

INTELLECT is NOT the most important thing in life ... It is the QUALITIES and VALUES which guide the emotions and the intellect, such as Goodness, Character, Love, Attitude, Heart and the Generous Qualities.

—Alfred A. Montapert

★ ★ ★

THE ROAD AHEAD

No one knows what is ahead.
The important thing is to use today
wisely and well and face tomorrow
eagerly and cheerfully and with
certainty that we shall be
equal to what it brings.

—Channing Pollock

★ ★ ★

WINNING

To be a winner in life, we must first be a winner inside. By that, we mean a solid foundation of high SELF-ESTEEM, SELF-CONFIDENCE, SELF-DISCIPLINE, CREATIVENESS and PEACE within.

We must have the VISION TO SEE, the FAITH TO BELIEVE, and the COURAGE TO DO. We WIN when we achieve our goals.

—Charles "Tremendous" Jones

★ ★ ★

LIFE GOES ON

No matter who goes, or who stays,
the world keeps on twirling.

—Alfred A. Montapert

★ ★ ★

SUCCESS QUALITIES

Experience has taught me that financial success, job success, and happiness in human relations are, in the main, the result of:

1. Physical well-being.
2. Constant effort to develop one's personal assets.
3. Setting up and working toward a series of life's goals.
4. Allowing time for meditation and spiritual regeneration.

—Roger Babson

★ ★ ★

CHEERFULNESS

Cheerfulness is the great lubricant of the wheels of life. It lightens labor, diminishes difficulties, and mitigates misfortunes. Cheerfulness gives a creative power which the pessimist never possesses. Use that strange power that comes with a cheerful laughing spirit. A cheerful disposition sweetens the day and smooths the road of life.

—Alfred A. Montapert

★ ★ ★

TRUTH

In sorrow he learned this truth ...
One may return to the place of birth.
He cannot go back to his youth.

—John Burroughs

★ ★ ★

THE UNIVERSE

Let man's first study be
the knowledge of the Nature
of the Universe.

—Lucretius

COMPLICATE

IF YOU MAKE A THING COMPLICATED ENOUGH,
NO ONE WILL UNDERSTAND
WHAT YOU ARE DOING TO HIM OR HER.

—Lawyer's Philosophy

★ ★ ★

VICTORY

The virtue of all achievement
is victory over oneself.
Those who know this victory
can never know defeat.

—A. J. Cronin

★ ★ ★

THE ANSWER

Strive for inner happiness,
regardless of circumstances.
WITH THE WORD OF GOD IN YOUR HEART
YOU HAVE THE ANSWER
for personal betterment!

—Alfred A. Montapert

★ ★ ★

USE OF TIME

TIME is the coin of your life.
It is the only coin you have ...
and only YOU can determine
how it will be spent.
BE CAREFUL, lest you let
other people spend it for you.

—Carl Sandburg

★ ★ ★

CHAPTER 6

MAN AND WOMAN

Family . . . . . Home . . . . . Marriage . . . . . Tact . . . . .
Personality . . . . . . Problems . . . . . . Service . . . . . .
Courage . . . . . . Obedience . . . . . . Principles . . . . . .
Appreciation . . . . Listening . . . . Maturity

---

DREAMS

A man is no greater than his dream,
    his ideal, his hope and his plan.
Man dreams the dream ... and fulfilling it,
    it's the dream that makes the man.

—Alfred A. Montapert

★ ★ ★

CHOICE

Nothing ranks people so quickly as their skill in selecting things that are really worthwhile. Every day brings the necessity of keen discrimination. Not always is it a choice BETWEEN GOOD and BAD, but often it is BETWEEN GOOD and THE BEST.

—Alfred A. Montapert

★ ★ ★

MANKIND

The Doctor sees all the WEAKNESSES,
The Lawyer all the WICKEDNESS,
The Theologian all the IGNORANCE.

—Schopenhauer

★ ★ ★

MAN'S FINEST HOUR!

The QUALITY of a person's LIFE...
is the RESULT of CONVICTIONS to high IDEALS,
DISCIPLINE of WORK and of PROBLEMS,
HIGH STANDARDS and CHARACTER,
FAITH in GOD and LOVE with COMPASSION:
COURAGE to fight LIFE'S BATTLES...
even with some defeats.

When he has done his BEST,
worked his HEART out for NOBLE CAUSES,
and lies battered and exhausted
on the field of battle—
THEN he is VICTORIOUS.

THIS IS MAN'S FINEST HOUR!
FOR TO BUILD A MAN...
IS LIFE'S GREATEST PROJECT—
FOR EACH OF US!

—Alfred A. Montapert

★ ★ ★

SOLUTION

A problem well stated,
Is a problem half solved.
State the problem well...
And you are half-way there.

—Charles Kettering

INHUMANITY

Man's inhumanity to man,
makes countless thousands mourn.

—*Robert Burns*

★ ★ ★

MAN WITHOUT GOD

Today, man's relationship with GOD is wrong. When man really sees that he ALONE cannot deal with evil and selfishness in human hearts, THEN MAN will wake up to find out what has REALLY wrecked ALL man's schemes.

—*Alfred A. Montapert*

★ ★ ★

THE DAY'S DEMAND

God give us men!
A time like this demands
Strong minds, great hearts,
True faith, and ready hand.

Men whom the lust of office does not kill;
Men whom the spoils of office cannot buy;
Men who possess opinions and a will;
Men who have honor; men who will not lie.

—*Josiah G. Holland*

★ ★ ★

FAMILY

When youngsters get into serious trouble, it is generally the parents who are delinquent, not the children. If you will look a little deeper, when some unpleasant incident occurs, you'll find that there's usually something wrong in the domestic menage. In too many cases, the parents are the ones who are in trouble and the parents are the ones who need help.

—*Walt Disney*

GREATNESS

No man is great in and of himself; he must touch the lives of other great people who will inspire, and lift, and push him forward.

—*Alfred A. Montapert*

★ ★ ★

EYES

THE EYES ARE THE WINDOW OF THE SOUL. LOOK AT THE PUPIL OF THE EYE AS YOU LISTEN TO A MAN'S WORDS! HOW CAN A MAN HIDE HIS WICKEDNESS IF YOU LOOK INTO HIS EYES? IF YOU WANT TO UNDERSTAND A WOMAN, WATCH HER EYES.

—*Charles "Tremendous" Jones*

★ ★ ★

CHARACTER

FAME will evaporate.
POPULARITY is a BURDEN.
RICHES take wings.
INTELLECT weighs as light as goose-
    down against the Gold of CHARACTER.
ONLY ONE THING ENDURES ... CHARACTER!

—*Richard W. Sampson*

★ ★ ★

BENEFIT

The writer does the most good
who gives his reader the most knowledge,
and takes from him the least time.

—*Sidney Smith*

★ ★ ★

COMMON SENSE

Thousands of engineers can design bridges, calculate strains and stresses, and draw up specifications for machines; but the great ENGINEER or ADMINISTRATOR is the man who can tell whether the bridge, or the machine, should be built at all; where it should be built, and when.

—*E. G. Grace*

★ ★ ★

BE YOURSELF

Don't ever apologize for your personality.
Do the best possible with what you have.
Insist on wearing your own hide.
INSIST ON BEING YOURSELF!

—*Alfred A. Montapert*

★ ★ ★

MARRIAGE

When you have EACH OTHER,
you have the greatest gift...
This is the greatest
of all God's blessings.

—*Alfred A. Montapert*

★ ★ ★

PURPOSE

The world turns aside
to let any man pass
who knows where he is going.

—*David Starr Jordan*

★ ★ ★

GIVE

No person was ever honored
for what he received.
HONOR has been the reward
for what he GAVE.

—Calvin Coolidge

★ ★ ★

FACE

The face is the mirror of the mind;
And eyes, without speaking, confess the
Secrets of the heart.

—Latin

★ ★ ★

ABILITY

Talent without TACT
is only half talent.

—Horace Greeley

★ ★ ★

IGNORANCE

IT IS IMPOSSIBLE
TO DEFEAT AN IGNORANT MAN
BY ARGUMENT.

—William McAdoo

★ ★ ★

OPINION

The more I see of man...
The more I like dogs.

—Madam de Staël

★ ★ ★

SELF-DESTRUCT

Know that men suffer under the evils
they have brought upon themselves.

—Pythagoras

* * *

GOSSIP

The person who gossips TO you,
Will gossip ABOUT you.

—Alfred A. Montapert

* * *

SILENCE

If you want others
To have a good opinion of you,
Say nothing.

—Blaise Pascal

* * *

TACT

Men,
like bullets,
go farthest when they are smoothest.

—J. F. Richter

* * *

MARRIAGE

If marriage is to be a success,
one should obviously begin
by marrying the right person.

—Hermann Keyserling

* * *

BRAVE

The brave deserve the lovely.
Every woman may be won.
And every woman wants to marry
A fine handsome millionaire.
But he is not going to pay
A million dollars for ten cents worth.

—*Alfred A. Montapert*

★ ★ ★

CONTENTMENT

In marriage, as in other things,
Contentment surpasses wealth.

—*Moliere*

★ ★ ★

MARRIAGE

Marriage does not consist of a big wedding.
TRUE marriage is a genuine HEART-UNION
of two people ... who become one ... forever.

—*Alfred A. Montapert*

★ ★ ★

SUCCESS

The road to success is filled with
women pushing their husbands along.

—*Lord Thomas Dewar*

★ ★ ★

THINK

You raise your voice when you should
reinforce your argument with FACTS.

—*Anthony B. Montapert*

DISCRETION

I have no enemy but myself.
IMPRUDENCE ... lacking discretion ...
this is my real enemy.

—*William D. Montapert*

★ ★ ★

THE SOFT ANSWER

"A soft answer turneth away wrath:
but grievous words stir up anger."

—*Solomon*

★ ★ ★

LIE

Sin has many tools,
But a LIE
Is the handle
That fits them all.

—*Alfred A. Montapert*

★ ★ ★

MAN

What man is before God,
that he is and no more.

—*St. Francis of Assisi*

★ ★ ★

POSSESSIONS

Who lives content with little
possesses everything.

—*Boileau*

★ ★ ★

LOVE AND MARRIAGE

The ultimate in life is to have a happy home with lots of love, peace of mind and contentment. Heaven couldn't be any better.

TRUE MARRIAGE IS A HEART UNION BETWEEN MAN AND WOMAN. The greatest project you will ever have in your whole lifetime is this relationship.

One of the deepest hungers of man's nature is for the experience and relationship of LOVE.

—Alfred A. Montapert

★ ★ ★

BEATRICE

Often, in my dreams, I have breakfast with you.
I sit beside you on your sofa.
I walk with you in your beautiful garden.
I embrace you daily in my thoughts a thousand times.

—Dante

★ ★ ★

HOSPITALITY

Many a man who thinks to found a home discovers that he has merely opened a tavern for his friends.

—Norman Douglas

★ ★ ★

HOME SWEET HOME

Every house where love abides
And friendship is a guest,
Is surely home, and home sweet home,
For there the heart can rest.

—Henry Van Dyke

★ ★ ★

PATIENCE

Before you meet a handsome
prince or princess ... you sure have
to kiss a lot of toads.

—Anon.

★ ★ ★

FOOL

There's a sucker
born every minute.

—Phineas T. Barnum

★ ★ ★

TROUBLES

It is easier to KEEP OUT of trouble
than GET OUT of trouble.
Most MISERY and TROUBLES
are caused by
LACK OF WISE THINKING beforehand.

—Richard W. Sampson

★ ★ ★

THE TONGUE

"Death and life are in
the power of the tongue."

—Proverbs 18:21

Be careful what you say—
you get what you order.

—Alfred A. Montapert

★ ★ ★

BE HAPPY

For every minute you are angry you have lost sixty
seconds of happiness.

—Emerson

MATURE PERSON

We would define a MATURE PERSON as one who is able to function happily, usefully, and at his maximum capacity in a given situation.

—*E. Stanley Jones*

★ ★ ★

MATURITY

The ability to handle the various phases of ordinary human life in an effective way, that is to say, in a way that produces a maximum amount of enjoyment and a minimum amount of stress, is what is known as MATURITY.

—*John A. Schindler*

★ ★ ★

BEST

You get the best
out of others
When you give the best
of yourself.

—*Harvey Firestone*

★ ★ ★

CRITICISM

Reprove a friend in secret,
but praise him before others.

—*Leonardo da Vinci*

★ ★ ★

SERVICE

No man is better than his SERVICE
for the betterment of others.

—*Candice M. Pope*

HOME

A HOUSE is built of logs and stone,
Of tiles and posts and piers:
A HOME is built of loving deeds
That stand a thousand years.

—Victor Hugo

★ ★ ★

SIMPLICITY

Life is not complex; we are complex.
Life is simple and the simple thing
is the right thing.

—Oscar Wilde

★ ★ ★

FAMILY

Don't get married unless you want to start raising a family, and don't start raising a family unless you want to get married.

—R. A. Lyman

★ ★ ★

TACT

Tact is the knack of making a point
without making an enemy.

—H. Newton

★ ★ ★

FANTASY

Creativity is not something reserved for artists, inventors or writers, but is inherent in all of us. Your fantasies can help you live life on several planes at the same time. A travel brochure on your desk can be the starting point for an imagined journey to some beautiful place.

—Around the World on the QE2

TALENT

Talent is common ...
Disciplined talent is rare.

—*William D. Montapert*

★ ★ ★

FAMILY and FRIENDS

Ships that pass in the night, and speak
    each other in passing,
Only a signal shown and a distant voice
    in the darkness;
So on the ocean of life, we pass and
    speak one another,
Only a look and a voice; then darkness
    again and a silence.

—*Longfellow*

★ ★ ★

GENIUS

Genius is not made for genius; it is made for mankind. Genius on earth is God giving Himself through man. Man is God's agent and, with His help, man does better than he knows. Each time that a masterpiece appears, it is a distribution of God that takes place. The masterpiece is a God-Man miracle.

—*Alfred A. Montapert*

★ ★ ★

PRINCIPLES

"All men, by natural intuition,
Feel and know common RIGHT and WRONG."

—*Aristotle*

★ ★ ★

HOME

HOME ... where each lives for the other
and all live for God.

—*Anon.*

* * *

HEART

She had a heart open to all ...
A real man wants a heart to himself.

—*Alfred A. Montapert*

* * *

SEX

Any fool can find sex ...
But only the wise find true love.

—*Alfred A. Montapert*

* * *

NOBLE PEOPLE

Remember this, that there is a proper dignity and proportion
to be observed in the performance of every act of life.

—*Marcus Aurelius*

DREAMS

I have learned this, at least, by my experiment; that if
one advances confidently in the direction of his dreams, and
endeavors to live the life which he has imagined, he will
meet with a success unexpected in common hours.

—*Henry David Thoreau*

* * *

GREAT MEN

The world's great men
have not commonly been great scholars,
nor its great scholars, great men.

—*Oliver Wendell Holmes*

★ ★ ★

SILENCE

Silence is golden:
The ability to speak several languages is an asset,
but to be able to hold your tongue in one language
is priceless.

—*Sydney Smith*

★ ★ ★

CLOSE-MOUTHED

He that keepeth his mouth, keepeth his life;
But he that openeth wide his lips
shall have destruction.

—*Solomon*

★ ★ ★

WORDS

How many a day has been dampened and darkened
by angry or careless words.

—*John Lubbock*

★ ★ ★

PEACE

He is happiest,
Be he king or peasant,
Who finds peace
In his own home.

—*Goethe*

IDEAL

I am an idea man ...
With Jesus Christ as my ideal.

—*Alfred A. Montapert*

★ ★ ★

LIVING

The art of living rightly is like all arts; it must be learned and practiced with incessant care.

—*Goethe*

★ ★ ★

WOMEN

He who is ignored by women
Is most fortunate,
For women are a trouble
And a worry.

—*Anon.*

★ ★ ★

BEST WAY

There is always a best way of doing everything,
even if it be to boil an egg.

—*Emerson*

★ ★ ★

ENTHUSIASM

Never allow your enthusiasm
To chloroform your judgment.

—*Alfred A. Montapert*

★ ★ ★

FREEDOM

He who has not learned to obey
can never be free.

—*Alfred A. Montapert*

★ ★ ★

OBEDIENCE

If you WILL stand in the rain,
why pray that God will keep you dry?

—*Dummy*

★ ★ ★

LISTEN

Benjamin Franklin said, *"I gave silence second place among the virtues I determined to cultivate. Considering that, in conversation, KNOWLEDGE was obtained rather by the USE of the EARS than of the TONGUE."*

★ ★ ★

MATURITY

The later years of life should properly be its crowning glory. Growth in stature and physical strength may cease at twenty-five, but head and heart, intellect, soul, and spirit keep on growing throughout the span of life.

—*Alfred A. Montapert*

★ ★ ★

PERSEVERANCE

Jim Corbett was asked, "What is the most important thing a man must do to become a champion?" He replied, "Fight one more round."

—*Anon.*

PERSONALITY

A combination of such desirable traits as optimism, cheerfulness, courage, poise, faith, decision, love, generosity, confidence, tolerance, and ability to mind one's own business will produce a very likeable man.

—*Charles R. Gow*

★ ★ ★

Personality is to a man
what perfume is to a flower.

—*Charles M. Schwab*

★ ★ ★

APPRECIATION

Don't be stingy with words of appreciation when they are justly due. Everyone likes to be told that he is admired, respected, and appreciated, and liked. Say "I like you because"—and be ready to give definite, specific reasons.

—*Alfred A. Montapert*

★ ★ ★

HOME

The home should be the best place we have going for us. It should be a place of peace, a place of refuge, a place of harmony, a place of beauty. The home has the greatest influence on the character of mankind.

Only LOVE ... PRIDE ... and DISCIPLINE ... make a
HOME.

—*Charles "Tremendous" Jones*

★ ★ ★

To be happy at home ...
Is the ultimate result of all ambition.

—*Sam Johnson*

WORSHIP

Man worships either God or an idol.

—Martin Luther

★ ★ ★

KINGS

Few men are fit
to wear a crown.

—La Fontaine

★ ★ ★

HOME

There is no place more delightful
than one's own fireside.

—Alfred A. Montapert

★ ★ ★

KNOW

"Man, know thyself."

—Socrates

★ ★ ★

WORTHLESS

A verbal contract isn't worth
the paper it's written on.

—Samuel Goldwyn

★ ★ ★

SPEAK TO ME

TO YOU! Stranger! If you, passing, meet me, and desire
to speak to me, why should you not speak to me? And why
should I not speak to you?

—Walt Whitman

THE POWER OF LAUGHTER

Few people realize that health actually varies according to the amount of laughter. People who laugh actually live longer than those who don't laugh.

—*Dr. James J. Walsh*

★ ★ ★

RETREAT

A great part of the happiness of life consists not in fighting battles, but in avoiding them. A masterly retreat is in itself a victory.

—*Longfellow*

★ ★ ★

ACCOMPLISHMENT

Lives of great men all remind us
We can make our lives sublime,
And departing, leave behind us
Footprints on the sands of time.

—*Longfellow*

★ ★ ★

DEATH

Death is a LAW
     Not a punishment.

—*Jean-Baptiste Dubos*

★ ★ ★

NEEDS

We seldom think of what we have, but what we lack. Man's needs are few, but his wants are many.

—*Alfred A. Montapert*

MARRIAGE

It is important not only to PICK the right mate, but to BE the right mate. Every man who is successfully married is A SUCCESSFUL MAN, even if he has failed in everything else. The highest happiness on earth is marriage.

—*Charles "Tremendous" Jones*

★ ★ ★

HOME

Home ... the spot of earth supremely blest.
A dearer, sweeter spot than all the rest.

—*Robert Montgomery*

★ ★ ★

PRIVACY

Make your home your castle. The most effective year-round release from rush and tension is in the home. That is, IF the sanctity of the home as a man's castle and personal retreat is preserved. When you can look forward to spending the evening in your peaceful family circle, with the draw-bridge up, it gives a glow and a more intense vitality to your whole day. Everyone will find it a lifesaver to build a schedule of privacy and stick to it at all costs.

—*Alfred A. Montapert*

★ ★ ★

CONTENTMENT

Most of us are more in need of a deeper sense
of CONTENTMENT with life as it is,
than we are of a deeper understanding of life.

—*Anthony B. Montapert*

★ ★ ★

CHAPTER 7

WORK

Toil . . . . *Occupation* . . . . *Business* . . . .
Loyalty . . . . . *Ethics* . . . . . *Humor* . . . . . *Hope* . . . . .

WORK

Every person's job is his life preserver. It is a law of Nature that when activity ceases, deterioration sets in. WORK is the grand cure of all the ills that beset mankind. Love your work and be happy, healthy and wealthy.

—Alfred A. Montapert

★ ★ ★

ACT

It takes more to plow a field
than merely turning it over
in your mind.

—Anon.

★ ★ ★

PLAN

No plan is worth a damn ...
unless somebody makes it work.

—Personal Planning Manual

★ ★ ★

BUSINESS

Leadership is earned ... not proclaimed!

—Charles "Tremendous" Jones

WORK

Thank God every morning when you get up that you have something to do that day which must be done, whether you like it or not. Being forced to work and forced to do your best will breed in you temperance and self-control, diligence and strength of will, cheerfulness and contentment, and a hundred virtues which the idle will never know.

—*Charles Kingsley*

★ ★ ★

BUSINESS

It is business, and business alone, both big and small, that keeps the American people working, clothed and fed. It is business that pays the salaries of both private and government workers. It is the goose that lays the golden eggs. The communist and socialist in our government must be voted out. We must remove over-regulations and return to free enterprise which is an open field of supply and demand.

—*Alfred A. Montapert*

★ ★ ★

ETHICS

Ethics means right human conduct. The assumption is that we should be concerned not only with our own welfare, but also with that of others. The compensation comes with satisfaction in doing "unto others as you would have them do unto you."

—*Louis Charbonneau*

★ ★ ★

HUMOR

When men get short of temper, HUMOR is a great solvent.

—*Felix Frankfurter*

★ ★ ★

LOYALTY

If you work for a man,
for God's sake, work for him.
If he pays you your bread and butter,
think well of him, speak well of him.

—*Elbert Hubbard*

* * *

WORK IS ESSENTIAL TO HAPPINESS

Life requires that we work (work being simply the opposite of rusting away) and nature requires that we work at something we were designed to do. Something that satisfies the soul. Such activity is exhilarating, interesting. It begets energy, health, and happiness. It defeats tensions and worry.

—*Anthony B. Montapert*

* * *

VALUES

Never is work without reward,
Or reward without work.

—*Livy*

* * *

LOYALTY

LOYALTY is rare, it is only proven under test.

If virtues could be graded, LOYALTY would stand near the top of the list. It creates a quiet confidence in the heart of any leader and is the assurance of success in any enterprise.

—*Alfred A. Montapert*

* * *

TO BUILD A MAN OR WOMAN

Far more important than what a man achieves is WHAT HE IS. TO BUILD A MAN IS THE GREATEST PROJECT ON EARTH. Men of genius are not nearly as important to civilization as men of GOODNESS. What men ARE is what makes them superior or inferior. It frequently happens that great intellectual ability is a curse because it is NOT accompanied by great integrity.

—*Alfred A. Montapert*

★ ★ ★

GROWTH

An acorn is not an oak tree when it is sprouted. It must go through long summers and fierce winters; it has to endure all that frost and snow and side-striking winds can bring before it is a full-grown oak. These are rough teachers, but rugged school-masters make rugged pupils. So, a man is not a man when he is created, he is only begun. His manhood must come with years.

—*Henry Ward Beecher*

★ ★ ★

ABILITY

The mark of an educated man is
the ABILITY to make a reasoned guess
on the basis of insufficient information.

—*A. Lawrence Lowell*

★ ★ ★

FUTURE

This is the kind of thinking you have to engage in: figure out what's going to happen in the future and figure out how you can participate in it.

—*William D. Montapert*

AN EXECUTIVE

Let me say right here, as strongly and emphatically as I possibly can, that the foundation stone of all executive ability is moral courage. If you have all the other qualifications—resourcefulness, personality, vision, technical knowledge, judgment, and all the mental speed in the world—and you lack the moral courage, the backbone, or, as it is vulgarly but expressively termed, the "guts" to make your own decisions on your own responsibility, you're no executive. I don't care what you're doing or how you're doing it. This is the heart of all executive ability.

—*Alfred A. Montapert*

★ ★ ★

PRODUCTIVITY

Degrees, doctorates, and fancy titles may help one get a job, but unless you can produce, they don't count for much. A man's worth to a company is his ABILITY to deliver.

—*Anthony B. Montapert*

★ ★ ★

STRUGGLE FOR PROFIT

The news media peddle PROFIT as a dirty word. The truth is that only profitable companies can provide jobs. Without the funds to modernize, invest in new products, build and expand, a company's future—and that of its employees and shareholders—is severely limited.

—*Charles "Tremendous" Jones*

★ ★ ★

WILLING

The world is full of willing people; some willing to work, the rest willing to let them.

—*Robert Frost*

MY DAILY DESIRE

To awaken each morning with a smile brightening my face ...
To greet the day with reverence for the opportunities it
 contains ...
To approach my work with a clean mind ...
To hold ever before me, even in the doing of little things, the
 Ultimate Purpose toward which I am working ...
To meet men and women with laughter on my lips and love
 in my heart ...
To be gentle, kind and courteous through all the hours ...
To approach the night with weariness that ever woos sleep
 and the joy that comes with work well done ...
 This is how I desire to waste wisely my days.

—Thomas Dreier

★ ★ ★

ADMONITION

Waste no time over vain regrets, losses or disappointments.
 Be grateful for present opportunities and privileges.
Bend your energies to the work that now lies before you.
 The remedy for worry, anxiety, and fears
 is to have new interests and responsibilities.

—Emerson

★ ★ ★

OUR BEST

The passing of a friend has just reminded me,
again, that my little day will soon be done. With the
sundown, may it be mine and yours to have the
assurance of both God and conscience that we have
done the best job that it is possible for us to do.

—Alfred A. Montapert

★ ★ ★

BUSINESSMAN

A man knocked at the heavenly gates, his face was scarred
    and old.
He stood before the man of Fate for admission to the fold.
"What have you done?", St. Peter asked, "to gain admission
    here?"
"I've been an executive, sir," he said, "for many and many a
    year."
The pearly gates swung open wide; St. Peter touched the
    bell.
"Come in and choose your harp," he said. "You've had your
    share of hell."

—Anon.

* * *

RELAX

Every now and then, go away, have a little relaxation,
for when you come back to your work your judgment will be
surer, since to remain constantly at work will cause you to
lose power of judgment. ... Go some distance away because
then the work appears smaller, and more of it can be taken in
at a glance, and a lack of harmony or proportion is more
readily seen.

—Leonardo da Vinci

* * *

HOPE

It is HOPE
which maintains most of mankind.

—Sophocles

* * *

BUSINESS

If you can swallow a toad every morning before breakfast, you are ready to do today's business.

—Old European Saying

★ ★ ★

Be Brief . . . .
       Be Bright . . . .
              Be Gone . . . .

—Alfred A. Montapert

★ ★ ★

QUALITY

Good buyers recognize quality
and the quality remains long after
the price is forgotten.

—Personal Planning Manual

★ ★ ★

HONOR

You can be deprived of your money, your job and your home, by someone else, but no one can ever take away your HONOR.

—William Lyon Phelps

★ ★ ★

DEFEAT

The WORST thing one can have
is a defeatist attitude.

—Alfred A. Montapert

★ ★ ★

SALESMAN'S SLOGAN

You have to tell them ... to sell them!

WORK OR WITHER

Aspiration, not content, is the Law of Life.
All life combines to make lazy men unhappy.
Work or wither is Nature's dictum.

The man we are, ought to shame us
into the man we ought to be.

—Alfred A. Montapert

★ ★ ★

HAPPINESS

Get your Happiness out of your work or you will never know
what Happiness is.

—Elbert Hubbard

★ ★ ★

LUCK

I believe in luck.
The harder I work ...
The luckier I get.

—Anon.

★ ★ ★

MASTER

We cannot be masters of a business
if the business is mastering us.

—Anon.

★ ★ ★

SUCCESS

Much as it may be decried, the cold fact remains that
ours is an economy actuated by profits. A certain return on
money is necessary to make our system work.

—Bernard Baruch

BUSY

It is not enough to be busy ...
The question is: What are we busy about?
—*Henry David Thoreau*

★ ★ ★

PERSONALITY

Make the most of yourself,
for that is all there is to you.

—*Emerson*

★ ★ ★

TROUBLE

There is nothing like work
to get your mind off your trouble.
—*Alfred A. Montapert*

★ ★ ★

PRAYER PLUS WORK

When I pray,
I pray like it all depends on GOD,
but when I get through praying,
I get up and work
like it all depends on me.

—*Dwight L. Moody*

★ ★ ★

SOLITUDE

To deeply THINK, CONCENTRATE,
and PRODUCE IMPORTANT WORK—
be alone ... isolate yourself ...
no distractions ... solitude ...
plenty of hush.

—*Alfred A. Montapert*

WORK

It is not sufficiently realized
that WORK is a great, if not the greatest,
FACTOR in keeping us well.

—Paul Dudley White, M.D.

★ ★ ★

HOPE

There is no medicine like HOPE,
no incentive so great,
and no tonic so powerful
as an expectation of something tomorrow.

—O. S. Marden

★ ★ ★

GIFT

Your talent is God's gift to you;
what you do with it
is your gift to God.

—Karl Malden

★ ★ ★

JOY OF WORKING

If You Enjoy Doing Something,
IT IS NOT WORK!

—Evelyn W. Montapert

★ ★ ★

DEEDS

We live in DEEDS ... not in years,
in THOUGHTS, not figures on a dial.
We should count time by heart beats.
He most lives who THINKS most,
FEELS the NOBLEST, ACTS the BEST.

—Philip James Bailey

INTELLIGENCE

The difference between
INTELLIGENCE and EDUCATION
is this:
INTELLIGENCE will make you a good living.

—Charles F. Kettering

★ ★ ★

BUSINESS

YES . . . . . . YES . . . . YES . . . .
BUT DID YOU GET THE ORDER?

—Alfred A. Montapert

★ ★ ★

PEOPLE

If the other planets are inhabited,
they must use this earth
as their insane asylum.

—George Bernard Shaw

★ ★ ★

FEE

A lawyer's time and advice
are his stock in trade.

—Abraham Lincoln

★ ★ ★

DEFINITION OF LAW

LAW is a rule of moral action
obliging to do that which is right.

—Grotius

★ ★ ★

ON TOMBSTONE

I told you I was sick!

—Anon.

OBJECTIVE

Set before yourself a great and definite life purpose. Hidden away in your innermost soul is a transcendent ideal capable of realization. What you need is not more capacity or greater opportunity, but increased resolution and concentration. Nothing will give you so much pleasure as the consciousness of making daily progress toward a great life purpose.

—Grenville Kleiser

★ ★ ★

ANGER

The greater the man,
The more restrained his anger.

—Latin

★ ★ ★

MAN IS UNIQUE

Nature arms each man with some faculty
which enables him to do easily
some feat that is impossible
to any other man.

—Emerson

★ ★ ★

WRITING

Nobody can make a motion picture great.
If it's not great on the written page,
it won't be on the screen.

—Mike Frankovich

★ ★ ★

CAN DO

He who can, does; he who cannot, teaches.

—George Bernard Shaw

PROGRESS

Problems are the price of progress.
Don't bring me anything but trouble.
Good news weakens me.

—Charles F. Kettering

★ ★ ★

YOUR RECORD

No matter what else you are doing,
　　From cradle days through to the end,
You're writing your life's secret story—
　　Each night sees another page penned.
Each month ends a thirty-page chapter,
　　Each year means the end of a part,
And never an act is misstated,
　　Nor ever one wish of the heart.

Each day when you wake, the book opens,
　　Revealing a page clean and white.
What thoughts and what words and what doings
　　Will cover its surface by night?
God leaves that to you—you're the writer.
　　And never one word shall grow dim,
Till someday you write the word "Finis,"
　　And give back your life book to Him.

—Wallace Dunbar Vincent

★ ★ ★

YOUR STATUE

Your life's work is your statue. You cannot get
away from it. It is beautiful or hideous, lovely or
ugly, or inspiring, as you make it.

—Alfred A. Montapert

CHAPTER 8

THE LAWS OF LIFE

Cause and Effect . . . . Action and Reaction.
Nature . . . . . Death . . . . . Change . . . . . Habit . . . . .

NATURE'S LAWS

Everyone in the Universe—as well as the Universe itself, including the Constellations, Nature, every Beast and Fowl, and every form of life, including Man—is governed by Nature's Laws. Man lives in Law as fish live in water. To know and obey is the secret of the wise.

—*Alfred A. Montapert*

★ ★ ★

NATURAL LAWS

There is a sense of solidity about the NATURAL LAWS which belongs to nothing else in the world. Here, at last, amid all that is shifting, is one thing sure; one thing outside ourselves, unbiased, unprejudiced, uninfluenced by like or dislike, by doubt or fear; one thing that holds on its way to be eternally incorruptible and undefiled. In these laws one stands face to face with truth, solid and unchangeable.

—*Henry Drummond*

★ ★ ★

CAUSE AND EFFECT

Today we are trying to CURE EFFECTS without finding FIRST CAUSES. We seem to have lost entirely the art of tracing EFFECT back to the prime FIRST CAUSE. That is the reason we never get anything cured or fixed.

—*Alfred A. Montapert*

BEST OF GUIDES

Live in accordance with NATURE.
Nature is the Best of Guides.
Obey her Laws and find Happiness.
Nature is the Handiwork of God.

—Alfred A. Montapert

★ ★ ★

CONTINUITY

When we observe the same thing happening every
day, we come to the conclusion that a Law of
Nature is involved ... such as the certitude that
there will be a tomorrow.

—Blaise Pascal

★ ★ ★

SMOKE SCREEN

Lawyers spend a great deal of
their time shoveling smoke.

—Oliver Wendell Holmes Jr.

★ ★ ★

TRUTH

He who speaks the TRUTH
speaks the LAW of
The Universe.

—William D. Montapert

★ ★ ★

LIBERTY

Liberty is the right to do
What the Law permits.

—Charles de Montesquieu

DISCOVERY

Napoleon could have ridden in an automobile. Shakespeare could have made "talkies" of his best plays. Caesar could have telephoned the news of his victories to Rome. Cleopatra could have had a steam yacht. Socrates could have recorded his dialogues on phonograph records. The principles on which all modern inventions are based, the materials out of which they are made, and the forces which operate them, *have always existed.* The world had to wait for a few men to discover and utilize them.

In the years before us, amazing inventions and improvements will be made in every line of work. Opportunities for fame and wealth await men of intelligence, imagination, and ingenuity who can perceive new or better ways to serve mankind, and put them into operation.

—*Kenneth S. Kleinknecht*

* * *

NATURE

NATURE is but a name for an effect,
whose cause is GOD.
The Universe is centered on GOD.

His infinite care is demonstrated
in the Cause and Effect,
Action and Reaction pattern
built into the Universe.

—*Alfred A. Montapert*

* * *

LIFE

Our lives are like a candle in the wind.

—*Carl Sandburg*

* * *

THE LAWS OF GOD

... are unseen forces which pervade and
govern the UNIVERSE and all therein.
They are never fully defined ...
only EXPERIENCED!

—*Alfred A. Montapert*

★ ★ ★

ETERNAL LIFE

For half a century I have been writing my thoughts in prose
and in verse—history, philosophy, drama, romance, tradi-
tion, satire, ode, and song. I have tried all. But I feel I have
not said the thousandth part of what is in me. When I go
down to the grave, I can say, like many others, "I have
finished my day's work!" But I cannot say, "I have finished
my life." My day's work will begin again the next morning.
The tomb is not a blind alley; it is a thoroughfare. It closes on
the twilight, it opens on the dawn.

—*Victor Hugo*

★ ★ ★

BELIEF

Your strong BELIEF that you CAN ... will bring results.
The Law of BELIEF will trigger the POWER which will impel
and carry your project to SUCCESS. THINK BIG, for you will
never be greater than your highest and best BELIEF and
ACTIONS.

—*Alfred A. Montapert*

★ ★ ★

EXPERIENCE

No one can be a good adviser until he has
his career behind him.

—*Napoleon*

NATURE'S LAWS

Nature's laws affirm instead of prohibiting. If you violate her laws, you are your own prosecuting attorney, judge, jury, and hangman.

—*Luther Burbank*

★ ★ ★

We live in a world of flowers and trees and grass, rivers and lakes and seas, mountains and sunshine. Nature is bright to the bright, comforting to those who will accept her comfort. Fresh air is as good for the mind as for the body. Nature always seems trying to talk to us as if she had some great secret to tell. And so she has .... .

—*John Lubbock*

★ ★ ★

Wake up and realize there is more to life than scientific progress, and a decay of the natural elements of living.

—*Bertrand Russell*

★ ★ ★

The fresh air of the open country is the proper place to which we belong. It is as if the breath of God were there wafted immediately to men, and a divine power exerted its influence.

—*Goethe*

★ ★ ★

One of the most satisfying experiences in life is a deep appreciation of nature. Wealth, health, families, friends, and fame can be taken from us but if we have a deep feeling for the beauty in nature, we can still be happy. Climb the mountains and get their tidings. Nature's peace will flow into you as sunshine flows into trees. The winds will blow their own freshness into you—and the storms their energy—while cares will drop off like autumn leaves.

—*John Muir*

JUDGMENT

On the Day of Judgment, when the trumpets sound
and we are finished with life on earth,
we shall be required to justify every word
that has carelessly fallen from our lips.

—Goethe

★ ★ ★

WHAT YOU ARE

Remember that WHAT YOU POSSESS
IN THE WORLD
Will be found at the day of your death
to belong to someone else,
But WHAT YOU ARE will be yours forever.

—Henry Van Dyke

★ ★ ★

BALANCE

A man should hear a little music, read a little poetry, and cultivate good thoughts every day of his life, in order that worldly cares may not obliterate the sense of the beautiful which God has planted in the human soul.

—Goethe

★ ★ ★

MORTALITY

Live mindful of how brief your life is.

—Horace

★ ★ ★

NEGATIVE

Thinking poor mouth
can make you poor.

—Anon.

UNSEEN FORCES

It is odd, when one thinks of it, that there are people in the world who, having renounced all the Laws of God and Nature, have themselves made laws which they rigorously obey.

—Pascal

* * *

QUALITY OF LIFE

The QUALITY of every person's life is DETERMINED BY THE KNOWLEDGE OF, and USE OF, the LAWS OF LIFE which are built into the very structure of man's nature. To discover and obey these laws is the highest of human enterprises.

—Alfred A. Montapert

* * *

MOVE AHEAD

Progress consists of learning
to apply laws and truths
that have always existed.

—John Allan May

* * *

TRAGEDY

There are NO tragedies ...
Just FACTS
NOT RECOGNIZED IN TIME.

—William D. Montapert

* * *

SELF-DESTRUCTION

Most people do not die naturally from old age.
They kill themselves prematurely
by their way of life.

—Alfred A. Montapert

ACTION and REACTION

With what measure you mete,
it shall be measured to you again.

—Matthew 7:2

*BE MORE AFRAID OF THIS LAW THAN OF CHAIN
LIGHTNING!*

—Alfred A. Montapert

★ ★ ★

FOLLY

Not even God can save a fool from his folly—
that is, from the result of his folly.
From the Law of Action and Reaction,
there is NO escape.

—Alfred A. Montapert

★ ★ ★

JUSTICE

There is one Universal Law that has been formed, or at least
adopted, not only by the majority of such and such a nation,
but by the majority of mankind. That Law is JUSTICE.
JUSTICE forms the cornerstone of each nation's Law.

—Tocqueville

★ ★ ★

INHERITANCES

How sad it is that when a man dies
His talents, skill, wisdom, or character
Cannot be inherited.

—G. G. Baumen

★ ★ ★

COMMON LAW

I sometimes wish that people
would put a little more emphasis
upon the OBSERVANCE OF THE LAW
than they do upon its enforcement.

—*Calvin Coolidge*

★ ★ ★

LAW OF LIFE

Things do not just happen, as many people think; they come to pass, and are the result of our thoughts, actions, deeds. If we make mistakes in life, we will pay the price. WE ARE THE ARBITERS OF OUR OWN DESTINY. THINGS WHICH WE ALLOW TO LODGE IN HEART AND LIFE ARE THE SEED, AND THE SEED WILL MATURE A HARVEST ACCORDING TO THE LAW OF "LIKE PRODUCES LIKE." The Law of Life is this: all seed must reproduce according to type.

—*Alfred A. Montapert*

★ ★ ★

NATURE

He that strives against NATURE
will forever strive in VAIN.

—*Samuel Johnson*

★ ★ ★

LIFE

The mintage of wisdom
is to know that rest is rust,
and that REAL LIFE
is in love, laughter, and work.

—*Elbert Hubbard*

★ ★ ★

MAN-MADE LAWS

There is a higher power and a higher law than the myriad of man-made laws that are causing man to have one foot on the other man's neck. Today we have an infinite network of man-made laws managed by a vast hierarchy of attorneys and politicians. Man has moved further and further away from nature and natural laws.

—Alfred A. Montapert

★ ★ ★

NATURE

Nature gives to every time and season
some beauties of its own.

—Charles Dickens

★ ★ ★

UNSEEN FORCES

ALL THE LAWS OF GOD ...
are never fully explained,
only experienced.
They are abstract but as real as the law of
gravity, and come to life when put to
personal experience.

—Alfred A. Montapert

★ ★ ★

DEATH

No mortal can escape death.

—Euripides

★ ★ ★

LIFE IS PRECIOUS

A man who dares to waste one hour of life has not
discovered the value of life.

—Darwin

POWER OF EXPECTANCY

We draw to us the things we expect.
EXPECT a VICTORY in advance.
Have the ATTITUDE of Positive Dynamic Expectancy.
FAITH is BELIEVING before receiving.
THINK and ACT like a WINNER.
Expect the BEST.
DESIRE and PERSISTENCE are the Driving Powers.
DYNAMIC EXPECTANCY—THE VICTORIOUS
WAY OF LIFE.

—Alfred A. Montapert

★ ★ ★

HABITS

It has often been said,
"What you are will determine what you do."
Not always.

You may be much better than your worst act,
and you may be much worse than your best act.
What you habitually do is you.

—A. P. Gouthey

★ ★ ★

BE A WINNER

Play the game of LIFE by the rules ...
The rules are the LAWS OF LIFE and GOD.
To LIVE ... BE ... and HAVE ... THE BEST,
We must follow the rules.

—Alfred A. Montapert

★ ★ ★

NATURE

"LIVE ACCORDING TO NATURE."

—Famous Greek Phrase

ETERNITY

Death is a doorway ...
NOT a wall.

—William D. Montapert

★ ★ ★

THE LAW OF DESTRUCTION

Everything has within itself the seeds
of its own destruction.
This applies to a person ... or a beast ... or a fowl
... or even a document.

—Alfred A. Montapert

★ ★ ★

CAUSE

There are a thousand hacking at the branches of evil,
to one who is striking at the roots.

—Henry David Thoreau

★ ★ ★

IRRITATION

If anything bugs you, get rid of it.

—Anthony B. Montapert

★ ★ ★

MAN'S LAWS

In a corrupt society, twenty million
laws can't succeed in enforcing the
Ten Commandments.

—William D. Montapert

★ ★ ★

MY LAWS

I will put My Laws into their minds,
and write them on their hearts.

—*Hebrews 8:10*

★ ★ ★

MORTALITY

Man, being mortal,
Cannot live forever.

—*St. Thomas Aquinas*

★ ★ ★

DEATH

All time is borrowed...
man is only a step from death.

—*Alfred A. Montapert*

★ ★ ★

PRAYER

Lead me from Falsehood unto Truth!
Lead me from Evil unto the Good!
Lead me from Death unto Immortality!

—*Hindu*

★ ★ ★

LAWS

Man's laws are man's way of dividing things.

—*William D. Montapert*

★ ★ ★

MEDIOCRITY

An epidemic of mediocrity is sweeping
the human race.

—*Walter Matthau*

NATURE'S LAWS

We know there is a Higher Power greater than we are. We see it every day in the daily law and order of the sun, the stars, the constellations, Nature and Nature's Laws. Man lives in Nature's Laws as fish live in water. This is the secret of the wise. Nature is the handiwork of God.

—*Alfred A. Montapert*

★ ★ ★

LAW OF CHANGE

Nothing is constant ...
Prepare for change.

—*Supreme Philosophy of Man*

★ ★ ★

NATURE

A goose flies by a chart upon which
the National Geographical Society
could never improve.

—*Oliver Wendell Holmes*

★ ★ ★

CHANGE

There is change in all things.
You, yourself, are subject to continual change,
And some decay ...
And this is common to the entire Universe,
Including the evolutionist.

—*Marcus Aurelius*

★ ★ ★

HABITS

Men's natures are alike;
it is their habits that carry them far apart.

—*Confucius*

* * *

LAWS OF THE UNIVERSE

If greater attention were given to the universal laws
which govern all forms of life, we would naturally mature
with a respect for the guiding agencies which reveal themselves in the operation of nature.

—*Manly Hall*

* * *

IN Nature, we recognize an infinite power.

—*Goethe*

* * *

IN Nature, there are neither rewards
nor punishments, there are consequences.

—*Robert Ingersoll*

* * *

MAN must go back to Nature for information.

—*Thomas Paine*

* * *

LIFE

For when the One Great Scorer comes
To write against your name,
He marks—not that you won or lost—
But how you played the game.

—*Grantland Rice*

* * *

MAKE YOUR LIFE BETTER

You can make your life better primarily by changing your mental attitude. Go through the family photo album, mentally reliving all the happy days you enjoyed together.

—*Alfred A. Montapert*

★ ★ ★

CONVICTION

The determining factor in effective communication is conviction. The authoritative voice that carries its message straight into the heart of every listener is that of the man who knows exactly what he believes. His utterance simply will not be denied, because it puts straight out from his spirit. Form does not matter. His sentences may not parse; he may commit crudities of pronunciation; his metaphors may lack polish, but people will listen with rapt attention because he believes so earnestly in his cause.

—*Clarence B. Randall*

★ ★ ★

INSPIRED

I have had quite a wide range of reading in the scientific field and have yet to find a real scientist who comes anywhere near touching bottom who has not a spiritual heart. When you get something that is worth reading you will get it from the pen of a man whose brain is inspired by something deeper down in him than his brain.

—*Alfred A. Montapert*

★ ★ ★

CHAPTER 9

SPIRITUAL FULFILLMENT

Prayer . . . . . .Meditation . . . . . .God . . . . . .Bible.
The Highest Power . . . . .Word . . . . .Faith . . . . .

THE HIGHEST POWER

Things go better when we are in harmony with—
The Divine Power that governs the Universe ...
The Supreme Power that governs Nature ...
The Unseen Power that heals Mankind ...
The Almighty Power that gives abundant
                    LIFE ... LOVE ... JOY
In GOD'S POWER, we live, move, and have our being.

—Alfred A. Montapert

* * *

INFINITE POWER

Among the mysteries which become more mysterious
the more they are thought about, there will remain the one
absolute certainty that we are ever in the presence of an
Infinite Power from which all things proceed.

—Herbert Spencer
World's Great Scientist

* * *

PRAYER ENERGY

If you make a habit of sincere prayer, your life
will be very noticeably and profoundly altered.

PRAYER is the most powerful form of EN-
ERGY that one can generate.

—Alexis Carrel, M.D.

DYNAMIC CHANGE

Only GOD'S DYNAMIC POWER can change the heart.

Our laws have inherently no dynamic power
to change anybody ...
the LAW OF THE LORD does.
The glory of the Gospel is ... IT CHANGES THE HEART.

Life truly begins with our supernatural rebirth.
Here is the greatest form of HAPPINESS, the greatest
SAFEGUARD, and the only thing that will
permanently satisfy the SOUL.

—Alfred A. Montapert

★ ★ ★

HIGHER POWER

I need to depend on someone who is bigger, stronger and
wiser than I am. I don't go it on my own. God is my strength.
He gave me a good body and some talent and the freedom to
develop it. He helps me when things go wrong. He forgives
me when I fall on my face. He lights my way.

—Hank Aaron
Atlanta Braves

★ ★ ★

DIRECTIONS

There is no EMERGENCY or NEED that can
possibly come into our lives for which the BIBLE
does not give DIRECTIONS.

—Alfred A. Montapert

★ ★ ★

SUPREME POWER

Looking up at the heavens and contemplating the stars,
what could be more obvious or clear than that some power of
superior intelligence exists that controls all these things.

—Cicero

POWER

The greatest thing
the greatest man ever did
was to pray!

—*Richard W. Sampson*

★ ★ ★

KNOW GOD

Some people have missed the most important thing in
life ... they don't know God:

And this is life eternal, that they might KNOW Thee, the only
true God, and Jesus Christ, whom Thou hast sent.

—*John 17:3*

To know is to experience.
To know is to fellowship.
To know is to enjoy.

—*Alfred A. Montapert*

★ ★ ★

FAITH

MIGHTY FAITH makes the heart full
of the POWER OF GOD.

The heart knows for CERTAIN that there is ...
"Nothing impossible to him that BELIEVETH."

Great FAITH, like muscles, develops with use.

—*Frederick K. Price*

★ ★ ★

COMPLETE FAITH

The world has yet to see what GOD can do
WITH and FOR and THROUGH and IN
a person who is fully and wholly consecrated to HIM.

—*Dwight L. Moody*

WHAT PRAYER IS

PRAYER is an ATTITUDE and a RELATIONSHIP ... powered by DESIRE.

Prayer is an ATTITUDE much more than it is anything else. An attitude of "My Father knoweth that I have need of all these things." Prayer is then an attitude of mind, an emotion of the heart, a companionship of my spirit with the Great Spirit.

PRAYER IS UNION WITH THE SUPREME POWER BY WHICH WE LIVE. God is my source—my source of birth, life, breath, comfort, strength, health, peace of mind, joy, love, faith and hope.

RELATIONSHIP: God abides within my soul—"The Kingdom of God is within." He is my best friend, a real personality which we call the Holy Spirit. Prayer is the tie between the individual and the Great Spirit. It is the human soul searching for this RELATIONSHIP.

DESIRE: Prayer is the soul's sincere DESIRE uttered or unexpressed. This desire can be great or small. Prayer connects you to the Higher Power. Men cannot live greatly without it. YOUR FAITH IS YOUR FORTUNE.

PRAYER is the key to Successful Living. Through prayer, I find God and God finds me. THE WHOLE ES-SENCE OF PRAYER DEPENDS UPON OUR FAITH. IT IS THE BELIEF THAT OUR HEART EXERCISES, THAT BRINGS RESULTS.

—Alfred A. Montapert

★ ★ ★

GENESIS

"In the beginning ... God."
This is the Alpha and Omega of LIFE!

—Bible

★ ★ ★

HOME

God is the home of the soul,
just as space is the home of the body.

—*Alfred A. Montapert*

★ ★ ★

LIGHT

Jesus said: "I am the light of the world.
The man that follows Me will not walk in the dark,
but he that follows Me will walk in the light."

—*John 8:12*

★ ★ ★

TRY TO SEE THE UNSEEN

It took me many years to realize that there are two realms ...
the Physical and the Spiritual. The things of the Spiritual are
UNSEEN. Very soon I learned to see the UNSEEN. Then I
had the right approach to the Spiritual Realm, and many
answers came to me. These were the things that were in the
Spiritual Realm and were eternal. For we walk by FAITH and
not by sight. *"For the things which are seen are temporal; but the
things which are not seen are eternal."* (II Corinthians 4:18.)

—*Alfred A. Montapert*

★ ★ ★

DIVINE POWER

I can do all things through Christ which strengtheneth me.

—*Philippians 4:13*

THE ONLY LIMIT TO THE POWER OF GOD LIES
WITHIN YOU!

—*Billy Graham*

★ ★ ★

VISION

"Where there is no vision, the people perish."
When men do not see from God's viewpoint,
they perish.

—Alfred A. Montapert

★ ★ ★

OBEY GOD

Fear God and keep His Commandments:
for this is the whole duty of man.
For God shall bring every work into judgment,
with every secret thing,
whether it be good, or whether it be evil.

—Solomon

★ ★ ★

HIGHER POWER

We plough the fields and scatter
The good seed on the land,
But it is fed and watered
By God's almighty hand.

—C. F. Kleinknecht

★ ★ ★

RIGHT

GOD'S UNIVERSE is geared to RIGHTEOUSNESS.
RIGHTEOUSNESS automatically writes its signature
across that which is RIGHT.

—Alfred A. Montapert

★ ★ ★

UNPARDONABLE

The UNPARDONABLE SIN is to shut God out of your
life.

—Alfred A. Montapert

IDEALS

Jesus Christ is man's highest ideal.
Ideals are like stars.
You will not succeed in touching them with your hand.
You choose them as your guides and, following them ...
you will reach your destiny.

—*Alfred A. Montapert*

★ ★ ★

FIRST THE KINGDOM

*"Seek ye first the Kingdom of God and His righteousness,
and all these other things will be added unto you."*
This constitutes the entire ministry of Jesus Christ.

—*The Bible*

★ ★ ★

DIVINE POWER

The great Supreme fact in human life, in your life and
mine, is coming into a conscious vital realization of our
oneness with the Infinite Life, and the opening of ourselves
to this divine inflow. As one comes into and lives continually
in the full realization of this oneness with the Infinite Life
and Power, all else follows.

—*Ralph Waldo Trine*

★ ★ ★

SUPREME POWER

We live in a universe of law and order. This means the
forces that guide the planets are governed by a dependable
Supreme Power. We can predict the appearance of a comet
fifty years hence, for the laws that govern the universe are so
dependable and accurate.

—*Supreme Philosophy of Man*

★ ★ ★

MY PRAYER

May God give me ...
TEARS ENOUGH to keep me tender.
HURTS ENOUGH to keep in sympathetic touch with those
who are in trouble.
FAILURES ENOUGH to make me ever aware of my depen-
dence upon God.
SUCCESSES ENOUGH to assure me that I labor together
with HIM.
And a spiritual experience that will enable me to always keep
first things in first place, so that when I come into the
Kingdom of God, I shall feel at home.

—*Alfred A. Montapert*

★ ★ ★

RELIGION

Real religion moves, inspires, compels, uplifts. Real
religion consists of feeling the indwelling presence of God,
not just reading about Him or reciting routine prayers
without feeling.

—*Rabbi Magnin*

★ ★ ★

ETERNITY

We are here not for a day, nor a week, nor a year. God
has set Eternity in our hearts. We are built on so vast a scale
that the years, be they multitudinous or few, cannot unravel
all the potentialities that God has packed within us. God did
build us especially for a million years.

And when the milleniums are grown weary with their
march and have fallen out by the way, we shall go on and on,
eternally on.

—*Alfred A. Montapert*

★ ★ ★

SPIRITUAL DEVELOPMENT

The first thing to develop is my SPIRITUAL
DEVELOPMENT.
This is the foundation stone of my life.
With this I can cope with life
and handle anything that comes my way.

—*Alfred A. Montapert*

★ ★ ★

BIBLE

The truth taught by the Bible is the right way to live.
Apart from the LIFE and TEACHINGS of JESUS,
life becomes an inexplicable mystery.
No marvel, then, that men who reject JESUS CHRIST
find life "not worth living."

—*Charles "Tremendous" Jones*

★ ★ ★

DYNAMIC FAITH

FAITH IS THE WHOLE ESSENCE—THE HEART OF THE
BIBLE.
FAITH is produced by knowledge and use of GOD'S
WORD.
FAITH is to BELIEVE and ACT according to GOD's
WORD.
FAITH IS BELIEVING BEFORE RECEIVING.

FAITH is a life-style ... God's Way of Living.
You limit GOD'S POWER in your life by your FAITH.

A Victorious Life depends upon YOUR FAITH!

—*Frederick K. Price*

★ ★ ★

CHRISTIANITY

Christianity is NOT a doctrine. It is not a creed that
we commit and live by rule and rote. CHRIS-
TIANITY IS A WAY OF LIFE. "FOLLOW ME" is the
command.

—*John L. Smart*

CONFIDENT LIVING

What is God's answer to this turmoil, this struggle, this life, this perplexity in which we live?

"Let not your heart be troubled."

Believe in God ... center your life in God. Times have changed, but here is a TRUTH that does not change:

The man who is centered in God is weaponed against any and every foe.

—Alfred A. Montapert

★ ★ ★

BLESSINGS

Every day that I live, I see more clearly ...
How all the POWER and BLESSINGS of the Christian life
Depend on one thing ...
KEEPING IN LINE WITH THE WORD OF GOD.

—Frederick K. Price

★ ★ ★

DISCIPLINE

A man devoid of religion
is like a horse without a bridle.

—Abraham Lincoln

★ ★ ★

VICTORY

With GOD'S WORD in your heart ...
each day is a VICTORIOUS DAY.

—Evelyn W. Montapert

★ ★ ★

TRUE RELIGION

While just government protects all in their religious rites,
TRUE RELIGION affords government its surest support.

—George Washington

MAN WORSHIPS OVER 3000 GODS

No man is an atheist. He worships some god or gods. If he does not subscribe to the Biblical statement of the Eternal God, he will create a god to which he will render his undivided allegiance. He may not "go to church" but he will, nevertheless, attend a church of his own making. He may call himself an atheist but he is, in reality, a devout believer. He may flatter himself that he does not "believe in prayer" but he is, finally, a devout man of faith.

He must worship SOMETHING. He is built that way. If not the God revealed in the Bible, then the gods of the State, Success, Money, Power, Fame, Education, Sex, Work, Laziness, Pleasure, Possessions, Gambling, Narcotics, Idols, Drunkenness, Gluttony, Pride. Of course, he does not call them "God," but they command the same devotion that a believer renders to the True God—and, alas, sometimes even more and better devotion. But the final hour of life will bring disillusionment. He will find that his god is too small and altogether inadequate.

—*Alfred A. Montapert*

* * *

EVIDENCE

Upon every face is written the record of the life the man has led; the prayers, the aspirations, the disappointments, all he hoped to be and was not—all are written there, nothing is hidden, nor indeed can be.

—*Elbert Hubbard*

* * *

THE HIGHEST GOAL

The end of learning is to know God and, out of that knowledge, to love Him and to imitate Him, as we may the nearest, by possessing our souls of true virtue.

—*Milton*

THE BIBLE—GOD'S WORD TO MAN

"This little volume," said the venerable Schliermacher, holding up a Greek New Testament before a group of English students, "contains more valuable information for mankind than all the other writings of antiquity put together."

The Bible is the foundation of all literature worth preserving. It is the central sun of the entire constellation of the world's best thought. From it all, human genius borrows its light. To it, human progress owes its greatest debt. It is the fountainhead of life and it reveals the best way to live and the only comfortable way to die.

Without the Bible, there is neither sense nor meaning to life. Have what we may, and get what we can, we shall have nothing and get only frustration unless we have and find Him. Modern life is only another name for muddled existence.

Again, the Bible stands alone when it comes to its power to transform character and life. Its strange white light searches the conscience and condemns the guilty. It smites like a hammer, burns like fire, cuts like a sword, and finally, leads the penitent gently to the Cross and there sheds its "beams around" him and whispers tenderest comfort into his broken heart.

Individuals have been transformed from criminals, thugs, gangsters and other worthless characters into worthy, strong and noble leaders. The hopeless, forlorn, sorrowing and defeated have found courage and comfort and confidence that they could have drawn from no other source.

Hold it tightly to your heart, for soon your little day will be done, and when the shadows lie deep across the west, it will hold your trembling hand and guide your unsteady feet through the sunset path into the presence of Him who breathed inspiration into the heart and mind of those who penned its sacred pages. Never, under any circumstances, allow yourself to be without it. Hide it in your heart, that you may not sin against God, and by so doing, fail to achieve your own highest good.

—*Alfred A. Montapert*

CHAPTER 10

PHYSICAL WELL-BEING

Health . . . . . . Diet . . . . . . Exercise . . . . . . Stress.

LAW OF HEALING

Healing is no accident. All nature heals itself when causes are removed and the conditions of health supplied.

> *Every living thing, from the tiniest plant to the grossest animal, repairs, replenishes, renews and heals its structures, or trends toward healing, even where death is inevitable as a result of overwhelming inimical influences and agencies, without the aid of artificial means, that life may be preserved.*
>
> *—Herbert Shelton*

★ ★ ★

SEVEN LAWS OF HEALTH

Eat live, natural, unprocessed foods, as much as possible. Good nutrition, exercise, rest, pure water, fresh air, sunshine and proper thinking are important factors in good health and well-being.

> *—Alfred A. Montapert*

★ ★ ★

LIFE

Life is only known as the complex of many functions,
and health as the integrity of these functions,
each in itself and their harmony among others.

> *—Peter Mere Latham*

HEALTH

HEALTH is our greatest asset—a precious thing.
Without HEALTH, pleasures, wisdom, love, life evaporate.
Good HEALTH must be earned and pursued
through exercise, diet, attitude,
discipline, self-control and goodness.

—Alfred A. Montapert

★ ★ ★

FASTING

Fasting is nature's way of curing illness. Observe the fasting practice of sick animals; they don't eat and they get well.

Alexis Carrel, the great scientist, wrote:

Privation of food at first brings a sensation of hunger, occasionally some nervous stimulation, and later the feeling of weakness, but it also determines certain hidden phenomena which are far more important. The sugar of the liver, the fat of the subcutaneous deposits are mobilized, and also the proteins of the muscles and the glands. All the organs sacrifice their own substances in order to maintain blood, heart and brain in a normal condition. Fasting purifies and profoundly modifies our tissues.

★ ★ ★

YOUR WAY OF LIFE

Walking is the one exercise you can follow all the years of your life. If there is one thing you can count on, showing up in the life histories of men who have lived to a great age in Good Health, that one "constant" is walking. Action absorbs anxiety ... helps take the stress out of life!

—Distilled Wisdom

★ ★ ★

VITALITY

Abounding health makes the eye sparkle, the step buoyant; one has the feeling of vim, vigor and vitality; it is a quality of the body that radiates; there is an inner sense of joy and gladness, consciousness of power accompanies it; it is plus vitality. Health is the first wealth.

—Essenes

★ ★ ★

OLD AGE

To me,
OLD AGE is 15 years older
than I am.

—Bernard M. Baruch

★ ★ ★

LEARN TO LIVE

Since you are NOT going to get out of this world alive, you might as well learn how to live in it as long as you can.

—Dr. H. J. Johnson

★ ★ ★

PREVENTIVE MEDICINE

It is extremely important to teach people how to prevent illness and disease. It is better to spend money on fresh air and sunshine, on gardens and vegetables. on orchards and fruits, on teaching exercise and right diets and nutrition. Also follow Nature's Laws of proper living. This is Preventive Medicine for your body.

—Alfred A. Montapert

★ ★ ★

"The sick man is too weak for the medicine."

HEALTH

The basis of all achievement is HEALTH.

—*O. S. Marden*

★ ★ ★

CHALLENGE

It is fascinating to know that one can grow healthier as one grows older—and not necessarily the reverse.

—*Dr. Paul Dudley White*

★ ★ ★

ADVICE

The ancient Greek physician-teacher Hippocrates, whose oath all doctors take, admonished:
1. Nature heals; the physician is only nature's assistant.
2. Thy food shall be thy remedy.
3. Meditation is for a man's spirit what walking is for his body.
4. Health can be found only by obeying the clear-cut laws of nature.
5. I shall keep my life pure and undefiled, and my art also.

—*Dr. Henry G. Bieler*

PHYSICIANS AND SURGEONS

I fear we are developing a group of competent technicians, treating disease, but not treating the whole patient.
All medicine is judgment. I can bring anybody in off the street and teach him how to cut and sew in three months.
It is knowing WHEN to operate and WHEN NOT to operate [that matters].

—*Alton Ochsner, M.D.*

★ ★ ★

HUMOR

Develop a sense of humor. This can be a most valuable asset. Have a good laugh every day, even if the situation is ridiculous.

—Anthony B. Montapert

★ ★ ★

AGE

It is our biological age that counts, not our chronological age. Our age is measured not in years, but by the manner in which we have spent our lives.

—Dr. Elton Morel

★ ★ ★

APPEARANCE

Would you like to be thin?
Yes, I would like to be ...
Thin, rich and young.

—Alfred A. Montapert

★ ★ ★

FAT

A fat paunch never breeds fine thoughts.

—Greek Proverb

★ ★ ★

OVERWEIGHT

Let's face it, the only sensible and safe way to reduce is to eat less and to eat the health-promoting foods. Systematic undereating and exercise will not only keep you slim but will also improve your health.

—Dr. Louis J. Klingbeil

TENSION

The Surgeon can cut out the ulcer,
but he can't cut out the tensions.

—*Dr. Alvarez*

★ ★ ★

ENERGY

The food you eat becomes your physical body ...
your bones, your hair, your skin, your teeth.
Your food supplies over 40 percent of your energy;
the other 60 percent comes from fresh air.

—*Alfred A. Montapert*

★ ★ ★

TENSION

Rid yourself of tensions:
Take a steam bath
Go for a walk
Take a swim
Practice yoga
Take a nice cruise
Go fishing.

★ ★ ★

RESPECT FOR YOUR BODY ...

Which is the only body you will ever have! Why must the physician see the patient only after he has gotten himself sick? The first thing doctors should teach their patients is respect for the human body and to begin to understand its functions better. Then begin to practice preventive medicine in order to enjoy health as well as to prolong life. "Dum Vivimus Vivamus ... while we live, let us live!"

—*Dr. Paul D. White*

OBESITY IS A FORM OF SELF-DESTRUCTION

FAT is your enemy. It plugs up the blood vessels, it increases your blood pressure and puts a load upon your heart. You feel uncomfortable and are a good candidate for illness and a short life.

"Obesity is an insidious killer that affects both the body and the spirit of its victim."

—*Dr. B. S. Howard*

* * *

TIME OUT TO FISH AND THINK

Relaxed attitudes are the means towards the GREATEST HAPPINESS as well as the greatest EFFICIENCY in life. Make sure you take time out (now and then) to FISH and THINK, and you will learn Serenity, and how TRANSITORY are human affairs.

—*Montaigne*

* * *

NATURE

You and your family must clearly understand that the GREAT AND ULTIMATE HEALER IS ALWAYS NATURE ITSELF AND THAT THE DRUG, THE PHYSICIAN, AND THE PATIENT CAN DO NO MORE THAN ASSIST NATURE, by providing the very best conditions for your body to defend and heal itself.

—*Sir Hans Krebs*

* * *

HEALTH

The more man follows nature and is obedient to her laws, the longer he will live; the further he deviates from these, the shorter will be his existence. Health is nature's reward for getting into harmony with her laws.

—*Anita Hesselgesser*

MENTAL ACTIVITY

Mental activity increases throughout adult life—IF the mind is kept active, interested and useful. It will decrease by inactivity, not by aging.

—Dr. Hardin B. Jones

★ ★ ★

LONG LIFE

Human nature longs for certainty in an uncertain world! There are no guarantees for you of a long life—but your chances of living a long while seem BEST if you come from a long-lived family, EXERCISE MORE and EAT LESS.

—Dr. Henry G. Bieler

★ ★ ★

CARELESSNESS

Carelessness about your way of life ... bad habits of all kinds ... bring on a host of troubles. When you break Nature's rules, YOU PAY, sometimes with your life!

—Alfred A. Montapert

★ ★ ★

STRESS

Our blood cholesterol goes up and down with our emotions. Most people get a few knots tied in their stomach due to the daily stress of today's modern living.

—Dr. Irving Page

★ ★ ★

HEART

A heart attack is an attack on your heart—by YOU!

—Hans Selye, M.D.

CHAPTER 11

MENTAL WELL-BEING

Thoughts . . . . Attitude . . . . Mind . . . . Brain . . . .
Power . . . . . Great Expectations . . . . . Fear . . . . .
Worry . . . . . Discouragement . . . . . Beliefs . . . . .

THOUGHTS

Whatsoever things are TRUE,
Whatsoever things are HONEST,
Whatsoever things are JUST,
Whatsoever things are PURE,
Whatsoever things are LOVELY,
Whatsoever things are of GOOD REPORT:
THINK on these things.

—Philippians 4:8

As a man thinketh IN HIS HEART, SO IS HE.

—Proverbs 23:7

★ ★ ★

YOU

The environment YOU fashion out of
. . . your THOUGHTS . . . your BELIEFS
. . . your IDEALS . . . your PHILOSOPHY
. . . is the only climate you will
ever live in.

—Alfred A. Montapert

★ ★ ★

BRAIN POWER

I use not only the brains I have,
but all I can borrow.

—Woodrow Wilson

POWER OF THE MIND

That the mind has great power over the body, there is not the slightest doubt. To consciously think that "I can " impels the subconscious faculties into action. Life is formed from the inside out. What I am inside determines the issues in the battle of life.

—*Dr. William Hornaday*

★ ★ ★

MIND POWER

"As I think, I am." Man's thoughts decide his destiny. Each of us creates his own life by his thoughts. Life is not determined by outward acts or circumstances. Here is the crux, the core of life: "As a man thinketh, so is he." So simple, but how true, how profound. How few understand and practice this law of man's nature: "As you think, you are."

—*Alfred A. Montapert*

★ ★ ★

THINK POSITIVE

Think optimistically and constructively. If anything seems to be wrong, take a brisk walk in the open air, breathe deeply, and affirm uplifting thoughts of ambition, strength, and prosperity. Cultivate the society of cheerful people. Read only pleasant subjects. Look for the BEST and HIGHEST things in life, and RESOLVE TO BE AN INTELLECTUAL OPTIMIST. Health, happiness, and prosperity are primarily mental.

—*Marian Ramsay*

★ ★ ★

LEARNING

First...we must tell a thing.
Second...we must illustrate it.
For we learn more through the eye
than we do through the head.

—Alfred A. Montapert

★ ★ ★

GO FORWARD

Finish each day and be done with it. You have done what you could. Some blunders and absurdities no doubt crept in; forget them as soon as you can. Tomorrow is a new day; begin it well and serenely and with too high a spirit to be encumbered with your old nonsense.

This day is all that is good and fair. It is too dear, with its hopes and invitations, to waste a moment on the yesterdays.

—Emerson

★ ★ ★

EXPECTANCY

To ACCOMPLISH great things, we must DREAM big
dreams,
then PLAN carefully and choose the proper METHOD.
We must not only ACT...but EXPECT.
The power of expectancy is tremendous.

—Alfred A. Montapert

★ ★ ★

VISUALIZE

Imagination is as good as many voyages...
and much cheaper.

—Anon.

★ ★ ★

BRIGHTEN YOUR DAY

One little kiss in the morning can reinforce the bond between husband and wife and provide a general feeling of well-being and health. This love and acceptance that people need contributes to relieve tension, to live longer, happier, and more successfully for both.

—*Evelyn W. Montapert*

★ ★ ★

ENCOURAGEMENT

When Napoleon created the Legion of Honor, he distributed thousands of crosses to his soldiers, made many of his generals "Marshals of France," and called his troops the "Grand Army." He was criticized for giving "toys" to war-hardened veterans, but his success and popularity were magnificent. This technique of giving encouragement, titles, and authority will work for you.

—*Fred Corbett*

★ ★ ★

ATTITUDE

The men whom I have seen succeed best in life have always been cheerful and hopeful men, who went about their business with a smile on their faces and took the changes and chances of this mortal life like men, facing rough and smooth alike.

—*Charles Kingsley*

★ ★ ★

GREAT FORCE

Our attitudes control our lives. Attitudes are a secret power working twenty-four hours a day, for good or bad. It is of paramount importance that we know how to harness and control this great force.

—*Tom Blandi*

HOW TO START YOUR DAY OFF RIGHT

To begin your day in a positive way, wake up your brain with some pleasant thoughts. While using my Exercycle, I think of all the pleasant things I could do today; such as, going to the beach, shopping for a suit, writing a letter, or calling someone on the phone. I can think of a thousand things to do, so I pick out the most important ones, then I happily go to breakfast.

—*Louis Charbonneau*

* * *

CONTENT

Very little is needed to make a happy life.
It is all within yourself—
in your way of THINKING and ATTITUDE.

—*Fred Corbett*

* * *

OPTIMISM

To live a long time and to enjoy life, the unseen force for you to develop is the PROPER ATTITUDE. The ability to deal with life in a RELAXED rather than a TENSE manner. I firmly believe this is the world's greatest need today!

HOW?

BANISH the NEGATIVE and your problems will melt away like icicles in a hot June sun. The cultivation of a cheerful, optimistic attitude and a firm Christian faith—"Belief in God"—is the basis for all health and happiness. Belief in the Supreme Power which is greater than you, will give rise to hope, and hope is one of the most powerful stimulants to which the body can be subjected.

—*Alfred A. Montapert*

* * *

PLEASANT THOUGHTS

Make yourselves nests of pleasant thoughts. None of us yet know, for none of us have been taught in early youth, what fairy palaces we may build of beautiful thoughts—proof against all adversity. Bright fancies, satisfied memories, noble histories, faithful sayings, treasure houses of precious and restful thoughts, which care cannot disturb, nor pain make gloomy, nor poverty take away from us—houses built without hands, for our souls to live in.

—*J. Ruskin*

★ ★ ★

PROSPERITY

Prosperity is a state of mind
which enhances every area of living:
HEALTH...WEALTH...HAPPINESS
Every day YOU write your own paycheck!

—*Alfred A. Montapert*

★ ★ ★

THOUGHTS

Here is the crux, the core of life:
AS A MAN THINKETH...SO IS HE.

Life is formed from the inside out. What I am inside determines the issues in the battle of life. Each of us must live off the fruit of his own thoughts. Our present thoughts determine success or failure in our work, study and daily living.

—*Dr. William Hornaday*

★ ★ ★

MIND

Man's greatness lies in his power of thought.

—*Pascal*

FEAR

Fear is the most devastating of all the human emotions. Fear hampers speech, paralyzes the faculties, can even cause a heart attack. You can conquer almost any fear if you will only make up your mind to do so. For remember, fear doesn't exist anywhere except in the mind.

—*Alfred A. Montapert*

★ ★ ★

PEACE OF MIND

This is the gift that God reserves for His special proteges.
Talent and beauty He gives to many.
Wealth is commonplace, fame not rare.
But peace of mind—that's His final reward of approval, the fondest sign of His love.
HE BESTOWS IT.
Most men are never blessed with it. Others wait all their lives—yes, far into advanced age—for this gift to descend upon them.

—*Joshua Liebman*

★ ★ ★

WEALTH

The glow of one warm thought,
is, to me, worth more than money.

—*Thomas Jefferson*

★ ★ ★

IDEALS

The power of ideals is incalculable.

—*Albert Schweitzer*

★ ★ ★

QUIET MIND

The best cure for the body
is a quiet mind.

—*Napoleon Bonaparte*

★ ★ ★

INSPIRATION

Thought inspired by love will yet rule the world.

—*William Jennings Bryan*

★ ★ ★

ASPIRATIONS

We have no aspirations because we
have no inspiration.

—*A. P. Gouthey*

★ ★ ★

WORRY

When I look back on all these worries, I remember the
story of the old man who said, on his death bed, that he had
a lot of trouble in his life, most of which never happened.

—*Winston Churchill*

★ ★ ★

CONFESSION

Why does God require confession of sin before there is
forgiveness? For the reason that until we are ready to face
and own up...that deviltry remains our own. Any psychol-
ogist will tell you that you can't get rid of what you won't
face. That's why the Bible says:

*"He that covers his sins shall not prosper; but whoso confesses
them and forsakes them shall have mercy."*

—*Proverbs 28:13*

GOOD THOUGHTS

Each day we need
GOOD THOUGHTS TO LIVE BY.
And remember...
You get what you order in life.

—Alfred A. Montapert

★ ★ ★

LAUGHTER

Laugh, and the world laughs with you;
Weep and you weep alone;
For the sad old earth
Must borrow its mirth,
But has trouble enough of its own.

Rejoice, and men will seek you;
Grieve, and they turn and go;
They want full measure
Of all your pleasure,
But they do not want your woe.

—Ella Wheeler Wilcox

★ ★ ★

REALITY

While I try always to "think positively," I also try not to delude myself as to reality.

—Alfred A. Montapert

★ ★ ★

CAPACITY

How much education is needed? It is a waste of time and effort to try to make lawyers, teachers, scientists, doctors, or preachers out of people who prefer and are better fitted to become foresters, mechanics, farmers, sailors, or chauffeurs. YOU CANNOT POUR FIVE GALLONS INTO A PINT CAN. THIS IS A LAW OF CAPACITY.

—Alfred A. Montapert

ATTITUDE

Have a happy, loving attitude. A positive attitude is mature health. This is the best state of psychological and spiritual health that can be obtained on this earth. HAPPINESS depends not upon things around me, but on my ATTITUDE. EVERYTHING in my life will depend on my ATTITUDE.

—Alfred A. Montapert

★ ★ ★

DIFFERENCE

It were not best that we should all think alike;
It is the difference of opinion
that makes horse races.

—Mark Twain

★ ★ ★

THINK

If you think you are beaten, you are:
If you think you dare not, you don't.
If you like to win but think you can't,
It's almost a cinch you won't.

If you think you'll lose, you're lost:
For out in the world we find
Success begins with a fellow's will:
It's all in the state of mind.

If you think you are outclassed, you are:
You've got to think high to rise.
You've got to be sure of yourself before
You can ever win a prize.

Life's battles don't always go
To the stronger or faster man;
But soon or late the man who wins
Is the man who thinks he can.

—Anonymous

STAY YOUNG

Nobody grows old by merely living a number of years.
It is the way you take care of yourself that counts.
Worry, stress, fear and despair bow the head.
Faith, courage, inspiration, love,
bring health, well-being and youth.

—*Alfred A. Montapert*

* * *

ATTITUDE

To be seventy years young
is sometimes far more cheerful and hopeful
than to be forty years old.

—*Oliver Wendell Holmes, Sr.*

* * *

THE BRIGHT SIDE

The right mental attitude means a great deal.
It is to the individual what the sun is to a plant.
It is worth a fortune to have the habit
of looking on the bright side of things.

—*The Way to Happiness*

* * *

DISCOURAGEMENT

You can tell how big a man is
by observing how much it takes to discourage him.
FAITH must overcome the onslaught of discouragement.

—*Alfred A. Montapert*

* * *

ELOQUENCE

Eloquence is the art of saying things in such a way that those
to whom we speak may listen to them with pleasure.

—*Pascal*

KIND

Lord,
help my words
to be gracious and tender today
for tomorrow I may have
to eat them.

—*Anon.*

* * *

GOSSIP

What people there are, Lord!
How great a number
of poisonous tongues.

—*Spanish Proverb*

* * *

MENTAL ATTITUDE

Listen to a football superstar, O. J. Simpson: "If you're going to be a superstar, in sports or anything else, it's your mind—not your body—that'll get you there.

"I believe success in any field is 70 percent mental. Sure, you have to have a certain amount of physical equipment before you can excel—but the key is the mind. It's concentration, the ability to blot out everything that doesn't help you do your best. You hear people talk about a person having 'heart' in sports. But what they're really talking about is mental attitude.

"You see people who spend their time on the bench even though they have better physical equipment and talent than a lot of the so-called 'superstars.' They just can't concentrate as well as the others."

* * *

CARING

Assume that every person you meet
has a sign around his neck which reads...
"Please make me feel important."

—*Distilled Wisdom*

* * *

THOUGHTS

If, this day, you were to read every page of every newspaper published in the world, you would find nothing more important to YOU than this:

1. YOU are the sole master of your thought processes!
2. "As a man THINKETH in his heart, so is he." Your head is the door to the heart. The head is the intellect, the Heart or Soul is the Spiritual Realm. The unbeatable combination is the individual with Head and Heart.

This is a law as real as the law of gravity.

—*Alfred A. Montapert*

* * *

ARGUMENT

If the subject is controversial,
please discuss it elsewhere.

—*Alfred A. Montapert*

* * *

DANGER

Negative thoughts are destructive.

—*Fred Corbett*

* * *

QUIET

The best thinking has been done in solitude.

—*Thomas A. Edison*

IMAGINATION

Imagination is more important than knowledge.

—*Albert Einstein*

* * *

PREPARE

Never do an important job or project
without ample preparation...
unless you deliberately want to fail.

—*Alfred A. Montapert*

* * *

FAILURE

Most FAILURES and MISERIES
can be traced directly back to
a lack of wise thinking beforehand.

—*Charles M. Simmons*

* * *

MENTAL DIVERSION

Try to keep your MIND constantly on the PLEAS-
ANT ASPECTS of life and on actions which can
improve your situation.
"Imitate the Sundial's way,
Count only the pleasant days."

—*Proverb*

* * *

STATE OF MIND

An OPTIMIST sees an opportunity
in every calamity;
A PESSIMIST sees a calamity
in every opportunity.

—*Herbert V. Prochnow*

SUCCESSFUL LIVING

What good is our present progress through technology and science if we fail to become better people? The fact is, that EACH OF US IS RESPONSIBLE FOR WHAT WE MAKE OF OUR OWN LIFE. The Government cannot play God, and create people who are identical in ability. This development is an INDIVIDUAL RESPONSIBILITY.

—Personal Planning Manual

* * *

THOUGHT

To speak without thinking
is to shoot without first taking aim.

—Spanish Proverb

* * *

FEAR

When you are established in righteousness,
you create a condition that overcomes fear.

—Alfred A. Montapert

* * *

MENTAL HEALTH

That the mind yields great power over the body has been known and proven for years. Your physical and mental and spiritual dimensions are all part and parcel of your being, and each one affects the other. There is a first cause for every effect, and the mind must be conditioned for health care and complete fitness of the total YOU.

—Alfred A. Montapert

* * *

EVERY PERSON BUILDS HIS OWN WORLD

There is one truth which we cannot appreciate too early or too well; namely this, that in the last analysis, every man lives in a world of his own making. The world in which we live is made up of the thoughts of our mind and the soul qualities. The environment YOU fashion out of YOUR thoughts ... YOUR beliefs ... YOUR ideals ... YOUR philosophy ... is the only climate YOU will ever live in. And as these qualities are very much within our control, it holds true that, in a very real sense, every man himself builds the world in which he lives.

So, whether the inner world in which he lives is one of difficulties, fears, doubt, gloom and despair, or of cheerfulness, sweetness and light, is the result of every person's own making. Whether we see the bright side of things or the dark, the hopeful or the ugly, the cheerful or the gloomy, is a matter, not of logic, but of habit of thought, habit of point of view, habit of interpretation; and the difference?—the difference between content and discontent, between happiness and misery, and, not infrequently, between prosperity and adversity, between success and failure.

It is commonly thought that happiness is a matter of worldly good fortune, but close observation indicates that outward circumstances have little to do with contentedness and peace of mind. We find, in this world, some men unhappy and miserable who apparently have everything that their heart can desire, while, close by, individuals who have nothing are the very embodiment of sunshine and happiness.

—*Alfred A. Montapert*

★ ★ ★

OPTIMISM

THE BEST IS YET TO BE...
The last of life
For which the first was made.

—*Robert Browning*

CHAPTER 12

LIFE

Experience . . . . . . Observation . . . . . . Social . . . . . .
Adversity . . . . . . Sorrow . . . . . . Friendship . . . . . .
Today . . . . Awareness . . . . Perceive . . . .

THE JOY OF LIFE

The true joy of life is being used for a PURPOSE that is only mine to fulfill. A PURPOSE which I recognize and BELIEVE to be a mighty one.

The joy of life is to give my best and be truly used in doing some good. My greatest passion is to be a creative force of Nature. I must do my noblest and walk hand in hand with God into the future ... into the forever

This is my duty for the Gift of Life.

—Alfred A. Montapert

* * *

LIFE

It too takes its rise in mystery, and like the little brook, begins its meandering journey down the canyon that we call years. Sometimes through sunny places, sometimes through shadowy, treacherous places, but ever going on, intent to reach some good.

—A. P. Gouthey

* * *

WELL-BEING

There are no riches above a sound body,
and no joy above the joy of the heart.

—Anon.

LIFE

The cost of a thing
is the amount of what I call LIFE
which is required to be exchanged for it,
immediately or in the long run.

—Thoreau

★ ★ ★

RAT RACE

We are all engaged in the rat race for worldly success. No one is exempt. Some are seeking money and possessions. Some are seeking power and fame. Some are seeking health and happiness. This whole enormous, costly, and constant effort to make some small mark on the great chessboard of life affects us all.

—Alfred A. Montapert

★ ★ ★

WEALTH

I don't want
to be a millionaire,
I just want
to live like one.

—Grovenor B. Montapert

★ ★ ★

AMBITION

I still find each day too short for all the thoughts I want to think, all the walks I want to take, all the books I want to read and all the friends I want to see. The longer I live, the more my mind dwells upon the beauty and the wonder of the world ... One's own door opens upon the wealth of heaven and earth ... Life is a struggle but not a warfare; it is a day's labor, but labor on God's earth, under the sun and stars, with other laborers, where we may think and sing and rejoice as we work.

—John Burroughs

FRESH AIR

There is nothing better
for the inside of a man
than the outside of a horse.

—*English Proverb*

★ ★ ★

REWARD

There is probably but one answer to the question "What do we get out of life?" And that is, "We get out of life exactly what we put into it," but we get that back in great abundance.

—*Alfred A. Montapert*

★ ★ ★

LIFE

Why should we leave the world
better than we found it?
Otherwise, there is no justification
for our existence.

—*Charles Gow*

★ ★ ★

SUFFERING

Nothing happens to any man
which he is not formed by nature to bear.

—*Marcus Aurelius*

★ ★ ★

PRINCIPLE
Work on the 3F Principle:
FRIENDLY...FAIR...FIRM.

—*Anon.*

★ ★ ★

WAY OF LIFE

We all have our own "way of life"...
Drinking is a way of life for some people -
Smoking is a way of life for some people -
Gambling is a way of life for some people -
Spending is a way of life for some people -
Complaining is a way of life for some people -
Worry is a way of life for some people -
T.V. is a way of life for some people -
Laziness is a way of life for some people.

Overeating is a way of life that I am correcting.
Exercising is a way of life that I am developing.
Proper attitude is a way of life that I am practicing.

Taxes are a way of life that reach us all.

—*Alfred A. Montapert*

★ ★ ★

MODERATION

Moderation, instead of excess,
is one of the most important words in the dictionary.

—*Napoleon Bonaparte*

★ ★ ★

DESTROYERS

Heroin, hashish, cocaine, opium, marijuana,
alcohol, nicotine, excessive stress or sex or worry,
are destroyers of mankind.
Addiction to any one is equivalent to suicide.

—*Alfred A. Montapert*

★ ★ ★

BE HAPPY

A Smile raises your Face Value.

—*Dail C. West*

A FOOL

Fool me once,
　　Shame on YOU.
Fool me twice,
　　Shame on ME.

—*Tom Blandi*

★ ★ ★

FAME

The constant pursuit of success and fame can eat up your whole life. You come to believe that you are more important than you really are. It is destructive to a person's existence.

—*Alfred A. Montapert*

★ ★ ★

THE GAME

You need enough money to live on
for food, shelter and raiment.
ABOVE and BEYOND that is just a GAME.

—*Alfred A. Montapert*

★ ★ ★

LIFE

Let us LIVE,
While we are alive!

—*Goethe*

★ ★ ★

EXPERIENCE

EXPERIENCE is our working capital.

—*Alfred A. Montapert*

★ ★ ★

DESTINY

Man has a destiny
to which all his life and activities
are directed.

—*St. Thomas Aquinas*

★ ★ ★

DECISIONS

Even now we can draw back...
but once we cross that little bridge,
we must settle things by the Sword.

—*Julius Caesar's words to his troops
as they prepared to cross the Rubicon*

★ ★ ★

TROUBLE

Some people are walking a tight rope
all of their life.
A few are doing it with a peg leg;
the rest are still on the rack.

—*Alfred A. Montapert*

★ ★ ★

ADVERSITY

You may not realize it when it happens, but a kick in the
teeth may be the best thing in the world for you.

—*Walt Disney*

★ ★ ★

VIEW FROM THE TOP

A well-ordered life is like climbing a tower; the view
halfway up is better than the view from the base, and it
steadily becomes finer as the horizon expands.

—*William Lyon Phelps*

BE GRATEFUL

During your lifetime there are people who have crossed your path who have helped you immensely. Thank God for these people, for they are as angels sent from Heaven. Give thanks for these dear ones from the depths of your heart, for their love and efforts have enhanced your life and made your journey happier and given you encouragement and satisfaction.

—*Alfred A. Montapert*

★ ★ ★

BOREDOM

There is nothing man finds so unbearable as being completely at rest, without passion, without business, without amusement, without purpose.

It is then that he recognizes that he is nothing, he is inadequate, powerless, empty, and far from independent.

Now pour forth from the depths of his soul, boredom, gloom, sorrow, chagrin, spite, and despair.

—*Pascal*

★ ★ ★

FROM THE HORSE'S MOUTH

I am always impressed when I hear people tell
what they HAVE PERSONALLY EXPERIENCED...
not something they read about or heard from others.

—*Paul Tournier*

★ ★ ★

RECREATION

Life is work, rest, and recreation,
and depending on that "recreation"
is the story of one's success or failure.

—*F. D. Van Amburgh*

LIVE

A wise old lady of eighty tells her friends as they reach sixty: "You have spent sixty years in preparation for life; you will now begin to live. You have conquered the worst forms of foolishness. You have reached a balance period of life, knowing good from evil; what is precious, what is worthless. Danger is past, the mind is peaceful, evil is forgiven; the affections are strong, envy is weak. It is the happy age."

—*Alfred A. Montapert*

★ ★ ★

SORROW

There is no sense in crying over spilt milk.
Why bewail what is done and cannot be recalled.

—*Sophocles*

★ ★ ★

GOLD AND GOODNESS

The great end of LIFE is GOODNESS.
Life is a battle...a test...and a reward.
When you combine GOLD and GOODNESS,
you have reached the highest plateau of living.

—*Alfred A. Montapert*

★ ★ ★

OLD AGE

Let us cherish and love old age
for it is full of pleasure...
if we know how to use it.

—*Seneca*

★ ★ ★

LIFE

I am come that you may have life.

—*Jesus*

Not a philosophy about life,
Not a set of do's and don'ts:
"I am come that they might have life."
This is His entire Gospel in epitome.
Everything He did and said centers here.

—*Alfred A. Montapert*

★ ★ ★

DESTINY

There is a destiny that makes us brothers.
None goes his way alone.
All that we send into the lives of others,
Comes back into our own.

—*Edwin Markham*

★ ★ ★

CONVERSATION

Never hold anyone by the button,
or the hand,
in order to be heard out;
for if people are unwilling to hear you,
you had better hold your tongue
than them.

—*Chesterfield*

★ ★ ★

FRIEND

Man's best support is a very dear friend.

—*Cicero*

★ ★ ★

LIFE

Life's greatest achievement
is the continual remaking of yourself
so that, at last, you know how to live.

—Winfred Rhodes

★ ★ ★

A FULL LIFE

Life is to be enjoyed,
to laugh, to sing, to love, to meditate.

—Alfred A. Montapert

★ ★ ★

FOOL

If a person calls you a fool, you are not a fool just because someone says so. The mere fact that someone says something does not mean that it is true. Many things people say are not true. You become a fool when you act like a fool.

—Anon.

★ ★ ★

CRIME

It is the crime which causes shame,
not the scaffold.

—French Saying

★ ★ ★

EXPERIENCE

Experience is a good school,
but the fees are high.

—Heinrich Heine

★ ★ ★

NO PAIN—NO GAIN

The greater the difficulty,
the greater the glory.

—Cicero

★ ★ ★

LIFE: ITS MEANING

The great use of a life
is to spend it for something that outlasts it.

—William James

★ ★ ★

LIFE UNDERSTOOD

Life can only be UNDERSTOOD—backward;
but it must be LIVED—forward.

—Soren Kierkegaard

★ ★ ★

MATERIALISM

Ours is a world of nuclear giants and ethical infants.
We know more about killing than we know about living.
We have grasped the mystery of the atom
and rejected the Sermon on the Mount.

—General Omar N. Bradley

★ ★ ★

FAIR AND SQUARE

Any society that takes away
from those most capable
and gives to the least,
will perish.

—Abraham Lincoln

ENHANCE

One of the important things to do in life is to enhance THE QUALITY OF EACH DAY, which is an art.

How is this done? In several ways...

1. Good thoughts to live by.
2. Congenial companions.
3. Good food. Taking loved ones out to lunch.
4. Work and accomplishment, which enhance each day and make it worthwhile.
5. Worthwhile entertainment.
6. Doing useful, creative and constructive work.
7. Serving and helping others.
8. Going to the beach...enjoying the sunshine and the fresh air.
9. Writing a letter to a loved one.
10. Smiling. Being a kind person.

—Alfred A. Montapert

★ ★ ★

DESPAIR

When we are flat on our backs,
there is no way to look—
but up.

—Roger W. Babson

★ ★ ★

TO WIN

I must FIGHT...if I would WIN!
You NEVER win a VICTORY...
without a BATTLE!

—Alfred A. Montapert

★ ★ ★

AWARENESS

Every child is born blessed with a vivid imagination. But just as a muscle grows flabby with disuse, so the bright imagination of a child pales in later years if he ceases to exercise it.

—Walt Disney

★ ★ ★

WORRY

It is better to SLEEP on things beforehand, than to lie awake about them afterwards.

—Baltasar Gracian

★ ★ ★

IDLENESS

The ruin of most people,
dates from some idle moment.

—G. S. Hillard

★ ★ ★

HEREDITY

Men are generally more careful
of the breed of their horses—and dogs—
than their children.

—William Penn

★ ★ ★

KNOWLEDGE

All you know for sure
is what you have experienced.
All the rest is speculation.

—Alfred A. Montapert

★ ★ ★

EVIL
No evil-doer can escape punishment.

—Greek Proverb

TRIALS

The gem cannot be polished
without friction,
nor man perfected without trials.

—*Chinese Proverb*

★ ★ ★

EXPERIENCES

It is the variety of experiences that makes life interesting. The human spirit thrives on alternations of toil and rest, pain and relief, hope and satisfaction, danger and security. If we remove the vicissitudes from life, it becomes an indolent and uninspiring affair.

—*Alfred A. Montapert*

★ ★ ★

ETERNAL LIFE

Life is real! Life is earnest!
And the grave is not its goal;
Dust thou art, to dust returneth,
Was not spoken of the soul.

—*Henry Wadsworth Longfellow*

★ ★ ★

LIFE

To see life as struggle rather than reward,
mental rather than environmental,
spiritual rather than material,
eternal rather than temporal,
is to move into a new mind and is to live
as a real person is meant to live.

—*John Homer Miller*

★ ★ ★

ADVERSITY

The tests of life are not made to break us. Trouble may demolish a man's business—but build up his character. The blow at the outward man may be the greatest blessing to the inner man. Adversity does not break men, it makes them.

—*Alfred A. Montapert*

★ ★ ★

LIFE IS A BATTLE

There are two great forces in this world—GOOD and EVIL; and no man is worth his salt unless he has lost and won battles for a principle. Life is a battle for what is right. No man lives without jostling and being jostled; in all ways he has to elbow himself through the world, giving and receiving offense. LIFE is a battle ... it is a fight from start to finish ... a struggle for survival from womb to grave.

—*A. P. Gouthey*

★ ★ ★

AWARENESS

Remember the A B C's:
Awareness
Before
Choice

—*Alfred A. Montapert*

★ ★ ★

LIFE

The longer I live the more beautiful life becomes.

—*Frank Lloyd Wright*

★ ★ ★

TEN STEPS TO BRIGHTEN YOUR LIFE

1. Begin the day in a calm and cheerful mood; say, "This is going to be a good day; I am going to be calm and cheerful—*right now*."
2. Try smiling at others—make believe your underwear is tickling you. A smile is contagious and you will feel better as others smile at you.
3. Count your blessings—list them one by one. Did you ever realize the real wealth you have?
4. Enjoy this day with beautiful thoughts, pleasant memories. Live life one day at a time.
5. Be adventurous. Try walking and see new neighborhoods, new buildings and parks, new scenery.
6. Give some friends a phone call or write a letter. Tell them you were thinking about them, encourage them; encouragement is oxygen to the soul.
7. Be a happy person, see the bright side of life, shun the gloom. Having a cheerful, loving attitude lends itself to your best health.
8. Do a good deed, buy a book, or give something beneficial to a loved one.
9. Give of yourself, offer your services to a hospital, to a church; help people. The law of giving will reward you tenfold.
10. Do the best you can each day; you are living only when you are useful and constructive.

—Alfred A. Montapert

★ ★ ★

YOUR OPTIONS

Experience is not what happens to you...
It is what YOU DO with what happens to you.

—Aldous Huxley

★ ★ ★

CAVEAT!

Fear not the Law...
but the Judge.

—Clarence Darrow

* * *

THE FOOL

The fool, with all his other faults,
has this also;
he is always getting ready to live.

—Epicurus

* * *

SACRIFICE

The road to the top is steep...
it is not cheap!

—Alfred A. Montapert

* * *

DIFFICULTIES

Men and women
owe the grandeur of their lives
to their tremendous difficulties.

—Alfred A. Montapert

* * *

WICKEDNESS

A wicked life leads to a wicked death.

—Moliere

* * *

GOOD DEEDS

How far that little candle throws his beams!
So shines a good deed in a naughty world.

—William Shakespeare

LIFE

The good life is one inspired by love
and guided by knowledge.

—Bertrand Russell

★ ★ ★

SIMPLICITY

Your life is what you make it.
Your life can be simple if you
will set it up with simplicity
as a goal. It will take courage
to cut away from the thousand
and one hindrances that make life
complex, but it can be done.

—Rhoda Lachar

★ ★ ★

EXPERIENCE

The knowledge of the world
is only to be acquired in the world.

—Chesterfield

★ ★ ★

LIFE'S MEASURE

Life is not dated merely by years.
Events are sometimes the best calendars.

—Benjamin Disraeli

★ ★ ★

EVENTS

I can trace my life through events.

—Alfred A. Montapert

★ ★ ★

CHAPTER 13

ACCOMPLISHMENTS

Goals . . . . *Leisure* . . . . *Adventure* . . . .
Travel . . . . *Inner and Outer Wealth*

ACCOMPLISHMENTS

During our lifetime, we are building a statue of our accomplishments. We are both the sculptor and the statue so we must be strong enough to take the blows of life. Some have no aspirations because they have no inspiration.

—Personal Planning Manual

★ ★ ★

WHAT IS INSPIRATION?

Inspiration is an invisible force within you that makes you feel good and inspires you to do things. Inspiration comes in all sizes; it may be small or large, but it is the catalyst that helps you to get things done. Inspiration is like muscles: the more you use them, the greater they are developed. Inspiration is the basis, the beginning, for all great accomplishments and enjoyments.

—Alfred A. Montapert

★ ★ ★

ACHIEVEMENT

The way to get things done
is to have a good assistant.

—William Feather

GOALS

In life, the FIRST thing you must do is decide what you really want. Weigh the costs and the results. Are the results worthy of the costs? Then make up your mind completely. Then go after your goals with all your might. You are living only when you are useful and accomplishing things.

—*Alfred A. Montapert*

★ ★ ★

TENDING TO BUSINESS

We attend to our business, and nothing else. You never heard of us on the road, nor driving four-in-hands. We never went to the theatre, but waited on those who did. We had no outside business, no ventures, no speculations in oil, wild lands, patents, or stocks. What money we had we put into our house. We took care of our business, and our business took care of us.

—*Delmonico*
Famous N.Y. Restaurateur

★ ★ ★

BE A MIRACLE

Do not pray for easy lives!
Pray to be stronger men.
Do not pray for tasks equal to your powers;
Pray for powers equal to your tasks.
Then the doing of your work shall be no
Miracle, but you shall be a MIRACLE.

—*Phillip Brooks*

★ ★ ★

TIME

Let us spend our days, redeeming the time, by quitting vain amusements, useless correspondence, those weak outpourings of the heart that are only modifications of self-love and conversations that dissipate the mind and lead to no good. Thus, we shall find time to serve God; and there is none well employed that is not devoted to Him.

—*Francois de Fenelon*

★ ★ ★

GOALS

You must have long-range goals
to keep you from being frustrated
by short-range failures.

—*Charles Noble*

★ ★ ★

ADVENTURE

Men grow when inspired by a high purpose when contemplating vast horizons. The sacrifice of oneself is not very difficult for one burning with the passion for a great adventure.

—*Alexis Carrel*

★ ★ ★

ACCOMPLISHMENT

When we finish one accomplishment
there is always another, then another. . . .
We never really arrive.

—*Personal Planning Manual*

★ ★ ★

SIMPLICITY

Abraham Lincoln was a man who cut through all the smoke and baloney and got to the core quickly and briefly. ... You don't have to know ten million things, just know the right thing. That is the secret of a farmer who has wisdom ... the secret of anybody who really has wisdom. You just know certain things well. That is what I call Essential Knowledge, meaning indispensable truth. I can live and die very successfully without knowing plenty.

—Alfred A. Montapert

★ ★ ★

MAKE UP YOUR MIND

To be ambitious for wealth, and yet always expecting to be poor; to be always doubting your ability to get what you long for, is like trying to reach east by traveling west. There is no philosophy which will help man to succeed when he is always doubting his ability to do so, and thus attracting failure. No matter how hard you work for success, if your thought is saturated with the fear of failure, it will kill your efforts, neutralize your endeavors and make success impossible.

—Baudjuin

★ ★ ★

ASPIRATION

Beware what you set your heart upon. For it shall surely be yours.

—Ralph Waldo Emerson

★ ★ ★

DESIRES

The significance of a man is not in what he ATTAINS, but rather in what he longs to attain.

—Kahlil Gibran

A HERO

An uncouth Tennessee mountaineer, a member of a religious sect opposed to war, many would have said was hardly worth the expense of equipping and sending overseas. Yet such a man, Sergeant Alvin C. York, was officially credited by Marshall Foch with the performance of the most conspicuous single deed of resourcefulness and courage in the annals of the whole stupendous conflict. Leading a squad of seven men, he killed or captured an entire German battalion, bringing in among the prisoners the major in command.

—*Alfred A. Montapert*

★ ★ ★

DEFEAT

What is defeat?
Nothing but education, experience.
It is defeat that turns bone to flint,
Fat to muscle, and makes men invincible.

—*John Lubbock*

★ ★ ★

TRAVEL

The advantages of TRAVEL last through life; and often as we sit at home some bright and perfect view of Venice, or Paris, London, Florence or Rome comes back to us and pleasant memories of days wisely spent in travel. I am a part of all that I have seen.

—*Around the World on the QE2*

★ ★ ★

WITHIN

Though we travel the world over
to find the beautiful,
we must carry it with us—or we find it not.

—*Emerson*

PLAN

God's plan for YOUR life....
The surest way to find yourself
Is to lose yourself in
Something bigger than yourself.

—*Alfred A. Montapert*

★ ★ ★

GLORY

Glory comes at the end,
Not at the beginning of life.

—*Alfred A. Montapert*

★ ★ ★

MEN

The world will never be better
than the men who inhabit it.

—*Joseph Fort Newton*

★ ★ ★

CONQUER INNER SPACE

As man conquers outer space, he seems to lose the conquest of self. In direct proportion as he masters what is outside of him, he seems to become enslaved on the inside. He has more room in which to stretch his muscles; he has less room in which to expand his soul. His thoughts dwell on orbiting the moon, but he himself has no orbit, no one thing around which he revolves. He knows how to control the universe; he does not know how to control himself. Sixteen out of twenty-one civilizations that have decayed from the beginning of the world until now did not succumb or fall through attacks from without; they fell by attacks from within by decay of the spirit.

—*Fulton J. Sheen*

SET YOUR OWN COURSE

What we are WITHIN registers itself WITHOUT. A river first digs a channel, then the channel controls the river. Men do not deliberately set out to become villains, drunks, thieves, drug addicts. They gradually become all these things by allowing themselves to become victims of the stream that cuts the channel of living deeper and deeper. We must form high ideals and good habits and control what channels are dug in our lives. The soul must become subordinated to high moral and spiritual ideals until at last such spiritual faculties become the dominating power in our life. Thus, and only thus, can any of us come to his highest and best and fullest living.

—Alfred A. Montapert

* * *

CAPACITY

We judge ourselves
by what we feel capable of doing,
while others judge us
by what we have already done.

—Longfellow

* * *

EXCELLENCE

Excellence in any department
can be attained
only by the labor of a lifetime;
it is not to be purchased
at a lesser price.

—Samuel Johnson

* * *

AMERICA

It is time for us to realize
that we are too great a nation
to limit ourselves to small dreams.

—President Ronald Reagan

★ ★ ★

ADVENTURE

Two roads diverged into a wood,
And I took the one less traveled by;
And that has made all the difference.

—Robert Frost

★ ★ ★

DIRECTION

The great thing in this world
Is not so much where we are,
But in what direction we are going.

—Oliver Wendell Holmes

★ ★ ★

LEADERS ARE READERS

You will be the same in five years as you are today; except
for the people you meet and the books you read.

—Charles "Tremendous" Jones

★ ★ ★

IMAGINATION

When I examined myself and my methods of thought,
I came to the conclusion that the gift of fantasy has meant
more to me than my talent for absorbing positive
knowledge.

—Albert Einstein

SINK OR SOAR

We will sink or soar
according to the choices which we make,
which choices eventuate into CHARACTER,
which CHARACTER ultimately will determine
whether we will sink or soar.

—*Alfred A. Montapert*

* * *

VICTOR HUGO

Victor Hugo rose above the clouds and gave to the world many masterpieces. He has passed on, but he is a living force. His works were based upon the Universal human heart, and so eternal. He was a friend of God.

—*Alfred A. Montapert*

* * *

CAUTION

Be cautious in your approach;
Show neither too little...
Nor too much zeal.

—*Horace*

* * *

MAN'S DIVINE DIMENSIONS

MAN has three divine dimensions:
Man has a body ... a physical being.
Man has a mind...a mental function.
Man has a spirit...a spiritual realm.
These three dimensions must function as a unit or man will be a glorious misfit.

—*Alfred A. Montapert*

* * *

UNPRODUCTIVE ACTIVITY

Do not mistake activity for achievement.

—*Mabel Newcomber*

★ ★ ★

WISHFUL THINKING

Some people think doctors can put
Scrambled eggs back into the shell.

—*Agnes M. Nelson*

★ ★ ★

THE WHOLE MAN

Man has a spiritual dimension and a mental dimension, as well as his physical dimension. It is wonderful to have a fine mind, this is a great blessing; BUT the unbeatable combination is HEAD and HEART. This is the WHOLE man—man at his best. Great men are men of head and heart.

—*Alfred A. Montapert*

★ ★ ★

GROWTH

Man is endowed with certain powers, faculties and abilities. Each man is responsible for their proper use, misuse, or neglect. It is each man's responsibility and duty to himself, to his world, and to the External Power to which he owes his existence, to develop these talents in keeping with the laws of his nature. In so doing he will learn to govern his temper, subdue his appetites, refine his emotions, inform his mind, and increase his understanding.

—*Manly Hall*

★ ★ ★

NOW

To do today's work well
and not be bothered about tomorrow
is the secret of accomplishment.

—*William Osler*

★ ★ ★

WORTHY ACTION

Count that day lost
Whose low descending sun
Views from Thy Hand
No worthy action done.

—*Josie Worth*

★ ★ ★

WINNING

Winning isn't everything...
But wanting to win is.

—*Arnold Palmer*

★ ★ ★

PERCEIVE

Hundreds can TALK
To one who can THINK.
Thousands can THINK
To one who can PERCEIVE.

—*Ruskin*

★ ★ ★

PASSION

For a man is a slave
to whatever controls him.

—*II Peter 2:19*

ASPIRATION

Lord, grant that I may always desire
more than I can accomplish.

—Michelangelo

★ ★ ★

DESIRE

"I'm modest. I just want to be champion."

—Hemingway

★ ★ ★

OUR ABILITY

One of the most healthy things in life is for each of us to
use the qualities Nature gave us, to the best of our ability,
and be satisfied and happy with what we can achieve.

—William C. Ross

★ ★ ★

CREDIT DUE

The credit for achievement goes to the person who does
things, not to the person who first thought of them.

—Anon.

★ ★ ★

WEALTH

Any man is wealthy who has good health, a happy
home life, a business or profession in which he is interested
and successful, a passion for growth, and the ambition to be
of service to his fellowmen. He could not get any more out of
life if he had a million dollars.

—Richard W. Sampson

★ ★ ★

WORTH

Nothing is worth more
than this day.

—Goethe

★ ★ ★

ETERNAL VALUES

ETERNAL VALUES are our wealth . . .
abiding things are our security.
God has tried in a thousand ways
to bring that truth forcefully to our attention.

—Alfred A. Montapert

★ ★ ★

FREEDOM

Have we too much freedom? Have we so long ridiculed authority in the family, discipline in education, rules in art, decency in conduct, and law in the state, that our liberation has brought us close to chaos in the family and the school, in morals, arts, ideas, and government? We forgot to make ourselves intelligent when we made ourselves free.

—Will Durant

★ ★ ★

TRUTH

There are two things in the Universe:
TRUTH, and THOSE WHO RESIST IT.

—*William D. Montapert*

★ ★ ★

MEN

Bring me men to match my mountains,
Bring me men to match my plains,
Men with empires in their purpose
And new eras in their brains.

—*Sam Walter Foss*

★ ★ ★

CHARACTER

Nature has written a letter of credit upon some men's faces
that is honored wherever presented. You cannot help trust-
ing such men. Their very presence gives confidence. There is
"promise to pay" in their faces which gives confidence and
you prefer it to another man's endorsement. Character is
credit.

—*Alfred A. Montapert*

★ ★ ★

QUALITY

The true test of civilization
is not the census, or the size of cities, or the crops,
but the kind of man that the country turns out.

—*Emerson*

★ ★ ★

HUMAN VALUES

Many people do not know what the HUMAN VALUES are.
Some of the true human values of life are:

Loyalty	Culture	Love
Gratitude	Balance	Truth
Achievement	Learning	Character
Moral Fortitude	Action	Happiness
Integrity	Goodness	Attitude
Solid Beliefs	Suffering	Honesty
Self-Esteem	Freedom	Discipline
Mental Health	Patience	Kindness
Confidence	Ethics	Health
Confessions	Leisure	Prayer
Contentment	Faith	Creativity
Friendship	Hope	Conduct
Moderation	Courtesy	Peace of Mind
Development	Beauty	A Sense of God
Human Relations	Pride	Responsibility

Live one day
At a time
And make it
A Masterpiece

—*Dail C. West*

★ ★ ★

PATIENCE

Patience and perseverance
have a magical effect
before which difficulties disappear
and obstacles vanish.

—*John Quincy Adams*

★ ★ ★

TRUTH

Man discovers truth through absurdity—through getting what he thought he wanted. In fulfilling his original dream, he comes to realize all the things money can't buy ... that, in the end, all any of us have is what we are in our relationship to other persons (love) and to ourselves (pride and principles).

—William D. Montapert

★ ★ ★

KINDNESS

I shall pass through this world but once.
If, therefore, there be any kindness I can show,
or any good thing I can do,
let me do it now;
Let me not defer it or neglect it,
for I shall not pass this way again.

—Stephen Grellet

★ ★ ★

PEACE

Nothing can bring you peace but yourself.
Nothing can bring you peace
but the triumph of principles.

—Emerson

★ ★ ★

COURTESY

Courtesy is the lubricant that eases the friction among human beings. Making other people feel good makes us feel good too. Try to act with LOVE for the feelings and well-being of others, then you will know how to be courteous.

—Alfred A. Montapert

★ ★ ★

ETERNAL VALUES

ETERNAL VALUES fix their own price,
and their QUALITY precludes all bargaining.
—Alfred A. Montapert

* * *

USEFULNESS

This is the true joy in life, the being used for a purpose recognized by yourself as a mighty one; the being thoroughly worn out before you are thrown on the scrap heap; the being a force of nature instead of a feverish little clod of ailments and grievances complaining that the world will not devote itself to making you happy.

—G. B. Shaw

* * *

HUMAN VALUES

Too many men who know all about financial values know nothing about human values.

—Roy L. Smith

* * *

OLD VALUES

Today we are afraid of simple words like *goodness* and *mercy* and *kindness*. We don't believe in the good old words because we don't believe in the good old values anymore. And that's why the world is sick.

—Lin Yutang

* * *

HONESTY

My Word Is My Bond.

—Motto of the London Stock Exchange

THINGS NOT WORTHWHILE

Some of the things in life that ARE NOT WORTHWHILE
are:

Envy	War	Despair
Greed	Violence	Unbelief
Hate	Fear	Gloom
Worry	Anxiety	Ill-Will
Murder	Revenge	Resentment
Negative Thinking	Riot	Jealousy

—Alfred A. Montapert

★ ★ ★

ENVY

Being resentful or jealous because of the good fortune of another ... there are no surer marks of littleness of mind and heart than a cold, critical, disparaging appraisal of the worth and success of others. Success is envy's hell. Failure in others is envy's heaven.

—Alfred A. Montapert

★ ★ ★

CONCEIT

We sure shook that bridge...
the mouse said
to the elephant.

—Anon.

★ ★ ★

IRREPLACEABLE

Every tooth in a man's head
is more valuable than a diamond.

—Miguel De Cervantes

UNJUST ATTACKS

It was very important for me to learn rather early in life Abraham Lincoln's attitude toward unfair criticism...

"If I were trying to read, much less answer all the attacks made on me, this shop might as well be closed for any other business. I do the very best I know how ... the very best I can; and I mean to keep doing so until the end. If the end brings me out all right, what is said against me won't amount to anything. If the end brings me out wrong, ten angels swearing I was right would make no difference."

How often men allow their energy to be dissipated and their good nature to be curdled by undue attention to baseless or unjust attacks.

—*Alfred A. Montapert*

EVIL

Evil is whatever does harm.

—*French Proverb*

★ ★ ★

TRUTH

I have searched for TRUTH early and late.
TRUTH is all I will have
when I come to the end of my little day.

—*Alfred A. Montapert*

★ ★ ★

FRUIT

By their fruits ye shall know them.

—*Matthew 7:20*

OUR HERITAGE

America's emblem is the soaring eagle,
not the blind and timid mole.
Fear, apologies, defeatism and cowardice
are alien to the thinking of true Americans.
As for me...I would rather be dead than Red.

—*J. Edgar Hoover*

★ ★ ★

TRUE GREATNESS

Today our big mistake is to think
of being GREAT without GOODNESS.
We place money and possessions in first place.
I wonder when the day will come
when a full head and a full heart
will count more than a full purse.

—*Alfred A. Montapert*

★ ★ ★

WORTH

A million dollars in the bank isn't worth a dime if the bank is closed. In other words, it's a good thing to develop reserves other than bank reserves; to accumulate riches that can't be taken from you. You'll find the accumulated riches of human experience in the great books. You can help yourselves to them. They're available in libraries; they aren't hoarded away or locked up in vaults. For years we've been trying to train our children to get rich. Most of them are still poor. Let's try training them to think.

—*William Benton*

★ ★ ★

STANDARDS

A thing that will help your inner life is to set up in your mind a standard of values, so that you know what is really significant, important, and valuable.

—*John Miller*

TRUTH

Never compromise a Principle
Nor relinquish a vital Truth

—Dail C. West

★ ★ ★

SUCCESS

We cannot have everything we want. The businessman in pursuit of financial success often has to neglect his athletic and cultural interests. Men who elect to serve the spiritual, the cultural, or the political interest of society—ministers, writers, artists, soldiers, teachers, statesmen, and public servants in general—usually have to relegate monetary well-being to secondary importance.

Michael Faraday never knew what it was to have a decent income, although he presented to the world a set of scientific discoveries the cash value of which to mankind has been estimated by Brailsford Robertson at some seventy-five billions of dollars. To Faraday's discoveries we owe the electric motor and the generator. Works of art that are now valued at hundreds of thousands of dollars were created in garrets while the artist was living on bread and water and giving the landlady arguments instead of rent.

Shakespeare, with his giant intellect, remained all his life one of the insignificant many, as far as the social and political life of his time was concerned. His soul and his heart were all in the art to which he had dedicated himself. Rembrandt, Voltaire, Rousseau, Wagner, Thoreau, Walt Whitman, all of them men of no mean ability, were poor, very poor. Money counted for nothing in their lives as against the vision that was drawing them on.

—Alfred A. Montapert

★ ★ ★

CREATION

If a man could make a single rose, we should give him an empire; yet roses and flowers no less beautiful are scattered in profusion over the world, and no one regards them.

—*Martin Luther*

★ ★ ★

DO YOU KNOW ME?

I am a little thing with big meaning.
I help unlock doors, open hearts, dispel prejudices.

I create friendship and good will.
I inspire respect and admiration.
Everybody loves me. I bore nobody.
I violate no laws. I cost nothing.

Many have praised me, none has condemned me.

I am pleasing to those of high and low degree.

I am useful every moment of the day, in many ways.
I am called "COURTESY."

—*Anon.*

★ ★ ★

THE RIGHT PERSPECTIVE

Ask not what your country can do for YOU; ask what YOU can do for your country.

—*John F. Kennedy*
Inaugural Address

★ ★ ★

COMPLAINTS

Sorry... yesterday was the deadline
for all complaints.

—Fred Corbett

* * *

ENVY

A friend was once complimenting the French Marshal
LeFevre upon his possessions and good fortune. There was a
certain ring of envy in his voice.

"You envy me, do you?" said the Marshal. "Well, you
shall have all these things, and at a better bargain than I had.
Come into the court; I shall fire at you with a gun twenty
times at thirty paces, and if I don't kill you, all shall be your
own."

The Marshal's friend was rather taken back at this.
"What! You won't?" continued LeFevre. "Very well; recollect,
then, that I have been shot at a thousand times, and much
nearer, before I arrived at the state in which you now find
me!"

* * *

PREJUDICE

You can't hold a man down
without staying down with him.

—Booker T. Washington

* * *

CURES

Go not for every ill to the physician,
Nor for every quarrel to the lawyer,
Nor for every thirst to the pot.

—George Herbert

* * *

SPIRITUAL VALUES

There is a growing realization in the United States that SPIRITUAL VALUES are·necessary to the survival of human society. Some degree of religious instruction must be restored to the public school system or the private schools will take over. Private worship will be restored in many families with beneficial results.

—*Alfred A. Montapert*

★ ★ ★

WELL DONE

God's *"Well done!"* is more important to me than the passing approbation of men who themselves have never known the true meaning of life.

—*Alfred A. Montapert*

★ ★ ★

CONCEIT

And so we plough along...
as the fly said to the ox.

—*Longfellow*

★ ★ ★

VALUES

Did you ever stop to think what would be the ideal life to live? Everyone should be given the opportunity to write it out, or give their expression. Let us see where our values are. We MUST have a set of values and live by them.

—*The Way to Happiness*

★ ★ ★

CHAPTER 15

FINANCIAL INDEPENDENCE

Money . . . . . . Investments . . . . . . Finance . . . . . .
Timing . . . . . . Risk. . . . . . Sacrifice. . . . . . Economy

MONEY

The real measure of a man's worth is how much he would be worth if he lost all his money.

—*Harold J. Smith*

★ ★ ★

MONEY

So, "MONEY," it is YOU who are responsible for life's anxieties, YOU who force us to take the road to early death; YOU who foster and encourage man's vices; the seeds of ambition spring from YOUR stock.

—*Latin*

★ ★ ★

INVESTMENTS

What are the ingredients of making money today? The answers are the same as they always have been. Desire, hard work, intelligence. Above all, an ability to LOOK AHEAD, which means loving reality, being pragmatic, and listening to what the markets are telling us.

—*William D. Montapert*

★ ★ ★

DIVIDENDS

The parable of the talents
is a lesson in investing.
You can NEVER receive a dividend
without an INVESTMENT.

—*Alfred A. Montapert*

* * *

MONEY

To make and preserve money,
one must have a plan,
based on sound facts and logical projections.
WITH A PLAN
you are a hundred times more likely to succeed
than you are without one.

—*Personal Planning Manual*

* * *

RICHES

I would have every man rich
that he might know the worthlessness of riches.

—*Emerson*

* * *

DEVELOPING A LIFESTYLE

Everyone is an individual, with different desires, tastes, and personality. Each must tailor his or her life to fit individual needs and tastes. You should decide NOW what you want from life. You are interested in going to Europe every year, having a place at the beach, owning a house, and having an art collection. And you can have them. I think that where we go wrong is that we try to get too much.

—*Alfred A. Montapert*

* * *

ACQUISITION

Ours is a money culture, there is no doubt about it, and there are large numbers of people in this culture who make acquisition, rather than enjoyment, the goal in life. They literally kill themselves in the greedy pursuit of more and more wealth. The idolatry of material success has infected all classes in our American society, and the inevitable failure of the vast majority of people to attain luxury and great wealth is responsible for the gnawing sense of insecurity and self-disdain.

—*Joshua Loth Leibman*

★ ★ ★

PROPERTY

Property is the fruit of labor;
property is desirable;
it is a positive good in the world.
that some should be rich
shows that others may become rich,
and, hence, is just encouragement
to Industry and Enterprise.
Let not him who is houseless
pull down the house of another,
but let him work diligently
and build one for himself,
thus, by example, assuring that his own
shall be safe from violence when built.

—*Abraham Lincoln*

★ ★ ★

FORTUNE

We mount to fortune by several steps ...
but require only one step to come down.

—*Stanislaus*

★ ★ ★

FORTUNE

Every man is the architect of his own fortune.

—*Latin*

* * *

INVESTMENTS

Everyone is interested in the proper and profitable use of money, which comes from two sources—EARNED INCOME and INVESTMENT INCOME.

Today it isn't a question of whether you want to invest or not. You MUST INVEST. Money is decreasing in value.

When you are young, make all the money you can and invest it so you will have the capital that will keep you in your later years. When you are young you should be "capital building," "estate building," so that as you become older you will be receiving a monthly spendable income from your investments.

You do not become wealthy on the money you work for. It is the *money that works for you* that makes the difference.

—*Alfred A. Montapert*

* * *

STOCKS

It's the only game in town where you can decide to get out as you pour yourself a cup of coffee and be out by the time you have finished drinking it. This is called liquidity, and it is worth an awful lot.

—*William D. Montapert*

* * *

FINANCES

A wise man does not trust all his eggs to one basket.

—*Cervantes*

MULTIPLY

Money breeds money.

—*Carl Sandburg*

★ ★ ★

FORTUNE

He has not acquired a fortune;
The fortune has acquired him.

—*Bion*

★ ★ ★

LIFE

FORTUNE and HUMOR rule the world.

—*La Rochefoucauld*

★ ★ ★

FORTUNE

Behind most every fortune, there is a crime.

—*William D. Montapert*

★ ★ ★

GOVERNMENT

No large private corporation could long survive if it practiced the waste and extravagance which is condoned in the Federal Government. Nor could the Government, if it were a competitive enterprise.

—*Herbert Hoover*

★ ★ ★

ADVERSITY

The flocks fear the wolf;
The ripe crops, the storm;
The trees, the wind; and
MAN the I.R.S.

—*Alfred A. Montapert*

MONEY

Can MONEY per se buy happiness? No!

Happiness depends upon our attitude. Negative attitudes destroy. Positive attitudes build self-esteem and character. However, we CANNOT live in this world without money. Money can buy comforts, time, leisure, books, nice homes, automobiles, and the things of this world ... but not happiness.

—*Alfred A. Montapert*

★ ★ ★

WHERE TO PUT YOUR MONEY

PUT YOUR MONEY IN SOMETHING YOU CAN USE AND ENJOY

After the home you need to live in, personal property (rugs, jewelry, art) are the ultimate investments.

—*William D. Montapert*

★ ★ ★

INVEST

Invest for TOMORROW
before your TODAYs slip away.

—*Alfred A. Montapert*

★ ★ ★

MONEY

He had so much money that he could afford to look poor.

—*Edgar Wallace*

★ ★ ★

MONEY

Isn't it amazing!
No man worth a million dollars ever gets old...
and the more he has the younger he looks.

—*Zsa Zsa Gabor*

REAL WEALTH

True wealth is what we become as persons ... what we are. What we possess is outside of us. WHAT WE ARE is an inner condition better than money. God gave everyone a bundle of gifts, and we are to develop these human resources, for that is where our real wealth lies. Goodness, Character, Confidence, are the generous qualities. FOR TO BUILD A MAN OR WOMAN IS LIFE'S GREATEST PROJECT ... FOR EACH OF US!

—Alfred A. Montapert

★ ★ ★

GREED

PRUDENT people get fed.
HOGS get butchered!

—Unknown

★ ★ ★

CHARLATANS

We have never lacked for
charlatans in this world.

—Jean De La Fontaine

★ ★ ★

BORROWING

Lending money to a man
makes him lose his memory.

—French Proverb

★ ★ ★

SACRIFICE

The path of glory
is a path of great difficulties and dangers.
Success calls for sacrifice.
The life of achievement is a life of hard work.

—Alfred A. Montapert

PRICES

Money serves as a common denominator which enables people to compare the values of many different things, ranging from a pound of butter to a trip around the world.

—*A. B. Zu Tavern*

★ ★ ★

MAN'S BUSINESS

Samuel Johnson said, *"Getting money is not all of a man's business. To cultivate kindness is a valuable part of the business of life."* It seems to me that the world today, in spite of its vast and costly educational system, is somehow lacking in teaching kindness and goodness and the art of consideration.

—*Louis Charbonneau*

★ ★ ★

POSSESSIONS

The most dominant force in the average person's life today is possessions. Learn to enjoy the money you make. Money is neither good nor bad, it is the use of it that falls into these categories. Money is the foundation of all successful business, but it takes more than money to make men rich.

—*Alfred A. Montapert*

★ ★ ★

SCAM

The darkest hour of any man's life is when he sits down to plan how to get money without earning it.

—*Horace Greeley*

★ ★ ★

Put MORE LIFE into your LIVING.

MONEY

Man is carnivorous; MONEY is the meat.
You cannot live in this world without money.
It is the USE OF MONEY that is important.

—William D. Montapert

★ ★ ★

IMAGINATION

"...if one advances confidently in the direction of his dreams
and endeavors to live the life which he has imagined, he will
meet with a success unexpected in common hours..."

—Thoreau

★ ★ ★

COMPOUND INTEREST

When asked to name the seven wonders of the world,
Baron de Rothchild once said: "I cannot. But I know the
eighth wonder is COMPOUND INTEREST."

It takes a little more than six years for money to double
at 12% return. Your effective rate of interest is actually over
20% because it's compounded. Through compounding, your
rate of return beats the present inflation rate.

—Alfred A. Montapert

★ ★ ★

ECONOMY

Economy is in itself a source of great revenue.

—Seneca

★ ★ ★

TIMING

TIMING is the key...to profitable investing.
You can be TOO EARLY or TOO LATE!

—Alfred A. Montapert

BORROWING

If you want to know
THE VALUE OF A POUND,
try borrowing one.

—*Spanish Proverb*

★ ★ ★

HANDLE WITH CARE

Money is the most dangerous stuff you will ever touch.

—*Alfred A. Montapert*

★ ★ ★

GAMBLING

There are two great pleasures in gambling:
winning and losing.

—*French Proverb*

★ ★ ★

GOVERNMENT

Public money is like holy water:
everyone helps himself.

—*Anon.*

★ ★ ★

PREMATURE

Never light the fire to fry the fish
before it is in the net.

—*Anon.*

★ ★ ★

THE PRICE OF FRIENDSHIP

He that has no money has no friends.

—*Anon.*

INSPIRATION

When we undertake a big work we have to do it with a large heart and a large mind. Small minds cannot undertake big works. When we see big works our stature grows with them, and our minds open out a little.

—Nehru

★ ★ ★

TIMING

TIME IS THE HEART OF ALL BUSINESS.
The big money is usually not made by the great prophets or seers. THEY SEE TOO FAR INTO THE FUTURE.
TO BE RIGHT TOO SOON
IS THE EQUIVALENT OF BEING WRONG.
In this regard, try to cultivate patience. After you've waited and things begin to happen is usually the perfect time to make your move. Most price rises have the following pattern:

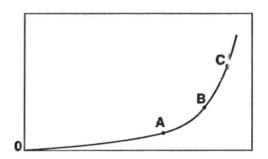

The ideal is to buy when the price is just moving from A to B. This way you avoid the long wait that O to A implies. Notice you are paying a higher price than at O, but it's worth it.

Another point to help you in your timing...
THINGS USUALLY TAKE LONGER TO HAPPEN
THAN IS GENERALLY SUPPOSED.
PINPOINT YOUR TIMING AND BE RIGHT!

—William D. Montapert

FULL MOON

Ah! The beautiful full moon.
Fat as a fortune!

—*Jules Laforgue*

★ ★ ★

GOODNESS

The greatest need in the world today is for people of sweet disposition, good character and harmonious nature.

—*Pearl S. Buck*

★ ★ ★

MISER

What good was her money,
since she deprived herself of everyting?

—*French Proverb*

★ ★ ★

WEALTH

Mankind's one objective is to amass wealth.

—*Pascal*

★ ★ ★

TROUBLES

For many men, the acquisition of wealth does not end their troubles ... it only changes them.

—*Seneca*

★ ★ ★

INHERITANCE

To all my friends,
I leave kind thoughts.

—*Comedian*

SPECULATOR

I am a speculator. The word comes from the Latin "speculari," which means "to observe." I observe.

—*Bernard Baruch*

★ ★ ★

CAVEAT!

Count your change
and your blessings.

—*Anon.*

★ ★ ★

CAREFREE

With much money and possessions come heavy responsibilities. The happiest and most carefree people are those who just have adequate. Solomon chose wisely when he said: *"Give me neither poverty nor riches."* Neither too little nor too much is the simple way of life.

—*A. P. Gouthey*

★ ★ ★

GOVERNMENT

Would it not be fine if our politicians, who, through taxation and regulations, do things to DESTROY and STRANGLE the independence of our best businessmen, would follow their example ... and give us better and better government at steadily declining costs?

—*William C. Ross*

★ ★ ★

BAIT

There is free cheese in every trap.

—*Yoshi Hamasaki*

IMPORTANT CAVEATS

We will never let our quest for profits interfere with hearing the music, tasting the foods, smelling the flowers or sleeping deeply at night. Above all ... let us never trade our health to make our wealth, or sacrifice too much time with our loved ones for little numbers on a page that will ruin our eyes and stultify our brains.

—William D. Montapert

★ ★ ★

COST

The cost takes away the taste.

—Alfred A. Montapert

★ ★ ★

MONEY

If wisely used, money may do much. Gold is power. Money gives us the means of acquiring what we wish. If fresh air, a good house, books, music, etc., are enjoyable, money will buy them; if leisure is an advantage, money enables us to take it; if seeing the world is delightful, it will pay for our journeys; if to help our friends, to relieve those who are in distress is a privilege, money confers on us this great blessing.

—John Lubbock

★ ★ ★

RISK

No one would ever have crossed the ocean if he could have gotten off the ship in the storm.

—Charles Kettering

★ ★ ★

CHAPTER 16

LOVE

Affection . . . . *Emotion* . . . . *Passion* . . . .
Memories . . . . . . *Noble* . . . . . . *Salutations* . . . . . .

LIFE

In this life we have three lasting qualities—FAITH, HOPE and LOVE. But the greatest of these is LOVE.

—*I Corinthians 13:5*

* * *

LOVE

LOVE IS DEMONSTRATION,
NOT MERELY DECLARATION.

—*Alfred A. Montapert*

* * *

GREAT PEOPLE

During your entire lifetime you will
meet only a few GREAT MEN and WOMEN.
Be careful how you treat them.
The monument of a great man is NOT of granite or marble or bronze. It consists of his GOODNESS, his DEEDS, his LOVE and his COMPASSION.

Angels come to visit us and we only know them when they are gone.

—*Alfred A. Montapert*

NEED

The greatest need of this day is LOVE.

—*Anon.*

★ ★ ★

KINDS OF LOVE

There are many kinds of love as many kinds of light,
And every kind of love makes a glory in the night.
There is love that stirs the heart, and love that gives it rest,
But the love that leads life upward is the noblest and the best.

—*Henry Van Dyke*

★ ★ ★

LOVE

The real value of love is the increased general vitality it produces.

—*Valery*

★ ★ ★

INSPIRING LOVE

It was Dante's deathless love for Beatrice
that gave rise to his sublimest thinking.

—*Alfred A. Montapert*

★ ★ ★

POSTPONED LOVE

Love is the greatest thing in the world. But we keep putting it off in our day-to-day living. We cannot make up today the damage we did yesterday by failing to love.

WE CANNOT LOVE RETROACTIVELY!

—*Alfred A. Montapert*

★ ★ ★

HEART

There are no little events with the heart.
It magnifies everything.
It places on the same scales
the fall of an empire...
and the dropping of a woman's glove;
and almost always
the glove weighs more than the Empire.

—*Honore de Balzac*

* * *

JEALOUS LOVE

There is no creature without love,
And no perfect love without jealousy.

—*Alfred A. Montapert*

* * *

KINDNESS

Love is kind, and kindness is love, in little things. The small words, "Please," "I'm sorry," "Excuse me," and "Let me help you," are love words used by all who practice kindness.

—*Evelyn W. Montapert*

* * *

LOVE'S OBJECT

Love is a dynamic attraction, far more powerful than atomic energy. We are shaped and fashioned by what we love.

—*Lou Charbonneau*

* * *

LOVE

Love comforteth like sunshine after rain.

—*William Shakespeare*

BROTHERLY LOVE

Jesus Christ came to this world to bring LOVE. The LOVE taught by CHRIST was the cement to bind all men together in brotherly love and kindness. But only a few practice His teachings.

—Alfred A. Montapert

* * *

THE GIFT OF LOVE

Our love is the greatest gift we can give one another.
"A bell is not a bell till you ring it.
A song is not a song till you sing it.
Love in your heart is not put there to stay.
Love is not yours—till you give it away."

—Oscar Hammerstein

* * *

POWER OF LOVE

What is love? I have met in the streets a very poor young man who was in love. His hat was old, his coat worn, the water passed through his shoes— and the stars through his soul.

—Victor Hugo

* * *

MISSION OF LOVE

Each one has a mission to fulfill,
a Mission of Love. At the hour of
death when we come face to face with
God, we are going to be judged on love;
not how much we have done, but how much
love we have put into our actions.

—Mother Teresa of Calcutta

* * *

A KING'S LOVE

But you must believe me when I tell you that I have found it impossible to carry the heavy burden of responsibility and to discharge my duties as King, as I would wish to do, without the help and support of the woman I love.

—*Edward VIII*
Abdication Speech

★ ★ ★

MANKIND

I am a mortal,
Born to love
And to suffer.

—*Friedrich Holderlin*

★ ★ ★

LOVE

Love's pleasure lasts but a moment;
The pain of love can last a lifetime.

—*French*

★ ★ ★

A WOMAN'S HEART

The most precious possession that ever comes to a man in this world is a woman's heart.

—*Josiah Gilbert Holland*

★ ★ ★

LOVE'S LIGHT

There is the same difference in a person before and after he is in love as there is in an unlighted lamp and one that is burning. The lamp was there, and it was a good lamp, but now it is shedding light too, and that is its real function.

—*Vincent van Gogh*

NOBILITY

There are many people who never wore a crown,
but are royal within.

—Anon.

★ ★ ★

EMPIRES

Alexander, Caesar, Charlemagne, and myself founded empires. But upon what did we rest the creation of our genius? Upon sheer force. Jesus Christ alone founded his empire upon LOVE, and at this hour, millions of men would die for Him.

—Napoleon

★ ★ ★

SOURCE OF LOVE

What is love?...It is the sweetness of life; it is the sweet, tender, melting nature of God, flowing up through his seed of life into the creature, and of all things making the creature most like unto himself, both in nature and operation.

—Isaac Pennington

★ ★ ★

HEART

Man's heart is a great rascal!

—French Proverb

★ ★ ★

LOVE

To love is to admire with the heart; and to admire is to love with the mind.

—T. Gautier

★ ★ ★

LOVE

To free himself of love,
A man need only concentrate
On his own problems.

—*Latin Proverb*

★ ★ ★

LOVE

Since we shall love each other,
I shall be great
And you rich.

—*Victor Hugo*

★ ★ ★

JEALOUSY

There is no greater glory than love,
Nor any greater punishment than jealousy.

—*Spanish Proverb*

★ ★ ★

LOVE

...The secret of Health, Happiness and Long Life: If you simply learn how to accept and express love, you will live longer ... be happier ... grow healthier. For love is a powerful force.

—*Alfred A. Montapert*

★ ★ ★

SUNSHINE

Love is to life what sunshine is to plants and flowers.

—*Tom Blandi*

★ ★ ★

SECRET LOVE

There is a name
Hidden in the shadow
Of my soul,
Where I read it
Night and day
And no other eye
Sees it.

—Lamartine

★ ★ ★

AMERICA'S YOUTH

We have taught our kids to demand American comforts, American privileges; to demand everything FROM America to make their lives easier. BUT ... we haven't taught them to LOVE America.

—Al Capp

★ ★ ★

HAPPINESS

The supreme happiness of life is the conviction that we are LOVED.

—Victor Hugo

★ ★ ★

ROMANCE

The most important step in life is marriage. Love seems to beautify and inspire all Nature. It raises the earthly caterpillar into the eternal butterfly; paints the feathers in spring, and lights the glow-worms' lamp. It wakens the song of birds, and inspires the poets' lay .

—John Lubbock

★ ★ ★

CHAPTER 17

WISDOM

Judgment ...... Reason ...... Acumen ......
Credo .... Honor .... Advice ....

WISDOM

Wisdom is the right use of knowledge. To know is not to be wise. Many men know a great deal, and are all the greater fools for it. There is no fool so great a fool as a knowing fool. BUT TO KNOW HOW TO USE KNOWLEDGE IS TO HAVE WISDOM.

—*Charles H. Spurgeon*

* * *

WISDOM

Perfect WISDOM has four parts:

Wisdom—the principle of doing things aright.
Justice—the principle of doing things equally in public and private.
Fortitude—the principle of not fleeing danger, but meeting it.
Temperance—the principle of subduing desires and living moderately.

—*Plato*

* * *

KNOW THYSELF

KNOW THYSELF...Wisdom is no more than the carrying out of this command.

—*Michel de Montaigne*

COMMON SENSE

Common sense
is NOT...
so common.

—Alfred A. Montapert

★ ★ ★

AWARENESS

There is something much scarcer,
finer and rarer than ability.
It is the awareness to recognize
ability.

—Robert Half

★ ★ ★

UNDERSTANDING

Happy *is* the man *that* findeth wisdom,
and the man *that* getteth understanding.

—Proverbs 3:13

★ ★ ★

ADVICE

A pretty safe rule to follow
is never to give advice until
you have achieved something
which qualifies you to advise...
then rarely give it.

—Alfred A. Montapert

★ ★ ★

PHILOSOPHY

Everyone has a philosophy
And your philosophy is what YOU BELIEVE;
YOUR eternal pursuit of Truth and Wisdom

—The Supreme Philosophy of Man

KNOWLEDGE

No knowledge we ever acquire is so important as a knowledge of what to say and how to say it; except, perhaps, a knowledge of what not to say, and when not to say it. Lee Du Bridge, former president of Cal Tech, says, *"The scientific man outside of his field is as dumb as the next guy."* We are all ignorant, only on different subjects. A college education does not make an educated man. THE TRUE TEACHER IS LIFE ITSELF, AND THE WORLD IS THE ONLY SCHOOL-ROOM IN WHICH WE CAN LEARN WHAT WE SO EVI-DENTLY REQUIRE.

—Alfred A. Montapert

★ ★ ★

QUARRELS

Wise Men
Do Not Pick Quarrels
With the Great

—Beaumarchais

★ ★ ★

IMPERFECT

There is a foolish corner
in the brain of the
wisest man.

—Aristotle

★ ★ ★

JUDGE

The first duty of a judge
Is to remember
That he is not GOD.

—Felix Frankfurter

★ ★ ★

SERVICE

There is no higher religion than
human SERVICE.
To work for the common good is the
greatest creed.

—Albert Schweitzer

★ ★ ★

WANTS

A man is rich
in proportion to the number of things
which he can afford to let alone.

—Henry Thoreau

★ ★ ★

FREEDOM

Modern man is the victim of the tragic conflict between law and human liberty. Liberty, like dynamite, is an efficacious but dangerous tool. We have to learn to handle it, and to handle it properly demands intelligence and will.

The frontier between the permissible and the forbidden is, as we know, invisible. Instead of wandering at will over the vast plain, we must keep to the track. And this track is narrow, rough and ill-defined. We must then voluntarily restrict our freedom if we are to succeed in life.

—Alexis Carrel

★ ★ ★

SIMPLICITY

Simplicity is making the journey of life
with just enough baggage.

—Charles Warner

★ ★ ★

MY DESTINY

God is my Father. Nature is my mother. The Universe is my way. Eternity is my kingdom. Immortality is my life. The Mind is my house. Truth is my worship. Love is my law. Form is my manifestation. Conscience is my guide. Peace is my shelter. Experience is my school. Obstacle is my lesson. Difficulty is my stimulant. Joy is my hymn. Pain is my warning. Work is my blessing. Light is my realization. Friend is my companion. Adversary is my instructor. Neighbor is my brother. Struggle is my opportunity. Future time is my promise. Equilibrium is my attitude. Order is my path. Beauty is my ideal. Perfection is my destiny.

—Harold Sherman

* * *

NATURE

NATURE understands no jesting. She is always true, always serious, always severe. She is always right, and the errors are always those of man.

She despises the man incapable of appreciating her, and only to the apt, the pure and the true, does she reveal her secrets.

—Goethe

* * *

SACRED MIRACLES

To me, every hour of the light and dark is a miracle.
Every cubic inch of space is a miracle.
If anything is sacred, the human body is sacred.

—Alfred A. Montapert

* * *

SEASONS

To everything there is a season, and a time to every purpose
  under the heaven:
A time to be born, and a time to die; a time to plant, and a
  time to pluck up that which is planted;
A time to kill, and a time to heal; a time to break down, and a
  time to build up;
A time to weep, and a time to laugh; a time to mourn, and a
  time to dance;
A time to cast away stones, and a time to gather stones
  together; a time to embrace, and a time to refrain from
  embracing;
A time to get, and a time to lose; a time to keep, and a time to
  cast away;
A time to rend, and a time to sew; a time to keep silence, and
  a time to speak;
A time to love, and a time to hate; a time of war, and a time of
  peace.

—Ecclesiastes 3:1-9

★ ★ ★

TRUE BIOLOGY

There are five kingdoms, each representing a stage in
life:
1. The mineral kingdom
2. The vegetable kingdom
3. The animal kingdom
4. The spiritual kingdom, or human kingdom
5. The Kingdom of God.

—Alfred A. Montapert

★ ★ ★

WISDOM

Real wisdom is looking at LIFE
From God's viewpoint.

—Alfred A. Montapert

PERCEIVE

I have made a ceaseless effort
not to ridicule, not to bewail,
not to scorn human actions,
but to understand them.

—Spinoza

★ ★ ★

JUDGMENT

Only judge when you have heard all.

—Greek Proverb

★ ★ ★

BECOMING WISE

There is a story frequently told of a Hindu chela who asked his master what a man had to do in order to become wise. The master took him into the Ganges and held the disciple's head under water for several seconds. "What did you think of while I was holding your head down?" asked the teacher. "Only one thing," replied the chela, "I wanted air." "How badly did you want air?" "More than anything else in the world." "Did you think of WEALTH, or REWARDS or AMBITIONS?" "No, master, only air." "Very well, my son, when you want WISDOM as you just wanted air, then you will become wise."

★ ★ ★

A WORD TO THE WISE

However beautiful...
or brilliant...
or rich you are...
you are likely to meet someone more beautiful,
more brilliant or richer than you are.

—Alfred A. Montapert

TEN MOST IMPORTANT WORDS IN THE DICTIONARY:

Moderation...   Character...
   Attitude...   Goodness...
      Thoughts...   Happiness...
        Health...   Security...
         Faith...   Love...

—Alfred A. Montapert

★ ★ ★

JUDGE

It is entirely easy to settle any question
if only one principle is involved.
But the hang of it is that most questions—
all questions that are difficult—
have a conflict of at least two, so-called, principles.

—Felix Frankfurter

★ ★ ★

REGRETS

Four things come not back:
the sped arrow;
the spoken word;
time past;
the neglected opportunity.

—Proverb

★ ★ ★

THE PHYSICIAN'S CALLING

The practice of medicine is an art, not a trade; a CALLING, not a business; a CALLING in which your heart will be exercised equally with your head. Often the best part of your work will have nothing to do with potions and powders, but with the exercise of an influence of the strong upon the weak, the righteous upon the wicked, of the wise upon the foolish.

—Sir William Osler

KNOWLEDGE

Knowlege is nothing else...
But perception

—*Plato*

★ ★ ★

RIGHT

It takes less time to do a thing right,
than it does to explain why you did it wrong.

—*Longfellow*

★ ★ ★

HONOR

Honor should take precedence over
Profit.

—*Anon.*

★ ★ ★

A CONSTANT SPRING OF PLEASURE

If man will but open his mind to the genius and spirit of
the world's great ideas, he will feel himself inspired with the
purest and noblest thoughts that have ever animated the
spirit of humanity.

—*Leon Gutterman*

★ ★ ★

WISE

Time ripens all things;
No man is born wise.

—*Cervantes*

★ ★ ★

INVEST

A wise man does not "spend"
his day, he invests it.

—*Personal Planning Manual*

RETICENT

Let another man praise thee,
and not thine own mouth;
a stranger, and not thine own lips.

—Anon.

★ ★ ★

JUDGMENT

Gentlemen—I have heard your opinions.
Some of you won't agree with what I say.
"I command a retreat."

—Napoleon

★ ★ ★

THE WISDOM OF GOD

The knowledge imparted by the Bible is wiser than the knowledge of the sages and infinitely more important than the speculation of the scholars. It is the wisdom of God that this hour needs to hear, more perhaps, than at any hour in human history. It is the directive that will map the course of action which alone can or will save us from the certain doom that now hangs over us as a result of our stupidity and neglect.

—Alfred A. Montapert

★ ★ ★

LEARNING

You Learn Up To Your Last Breath.

—Alfred A. Montapert

★ ★ ★

TRUE WISDOM

A loving heart is the truest wisdom.

—Charles Dickens

CHAPTER 18

TODAY'S WORLD

Government . . . . *Politicians* . . . . *Lawyers*

OPTIMISM

I hold not with the pessimist that all things are ill, nor with the optimist that all things are well. All things are not well, but all things shall be well, because this is God's world.

—*Robert Browning*

★ ★ ★

TODAY'S WORLD

There is no need to lament the modern world. The TODAY it offers is the only one we have and we must learn to make the most of it. We must learn TO LIVE with the problems and absurdities that we now face; even use them to make a good living for ourselves and our families.

—*Alfred A. Montapert*

★ ★ ★

REALITY

This is a cold world in which we live. It is coldly calculating, frigidly selfish, freezingly thoughtless, and frostily unconcerned. Life is a battle. You are fighting every day to stay alive; to exist physically, mentally, emotionally, financially and socially.

—*Alfred A. Montapert*

TODAY'S WORLD

More than two thousand years ago, Plato argued that democracy would destroy itself because the masses were selfish and would push the government into actions that might hurt society as a whole.

That is exactly what has been happening in America for the last fifty years. A generation of Congressmen grew up anxious to respond to all of life's problems by throwing money at them.

Federal social spending has soared from 89 billion in 1971 to 349 billion this fiscal year. When the food stamp program began, only one American in 492 qualified; now, one is six is eligible.

If we as a nation persist in the direction we're going, we will eventually reach the riot-point ... the stage where disaffected people simply won't take it anymore and take to the streets instead.

—Richard W. Sampson

★ ★ ★

GOVERNMENT

Dedicated statesmen made this Nation great...
But now we are letting liberal politicians destroy it.
Both our money and our morals.
We have compromised Principle and Truth for trash.
Our liberalism has blinded our virtues and duty,
Destroyed our morals and basic principles.

—Jack E. Gould

★ ★ ★

RAPID CHANGE

We live in a world in which the speed of change is so swift that it is greater than at any other period in its history. Most of our problems arise from this fact ... the speed of change.

—Hal Leighton

INFLUENCE

The influence of a man's life lives on whether he is alive or dead, whether it is good or evil. We are all responsible for our influence. The influence of great men will live on through the centuries.

—*The Way to Happiness*

* * *

OUR PRESENT SITUATION

So here we are in the nineteen-eighties, searching for ways by which we can bring back the essential principles of living. The effects of our age of materialism, misdirection, misunderstanding and misinterpretation, the failure of the individual to elevate the GOLDEN RULE above the sciences which we cultivated for industrial purposes, and the failure of man to think straight, are all coming home to bug man.

With God's continued blessings and provision, we are optimistic about the nineteen-eighties. While many are crying and fighting for survival, we are smiling and looking ahead at all the challenges and opportunities. Our trust and hope is in God ... who could ask for more?

—*Alfred A. Montapert*

* * *

MY PARTING ADMONITION

Let shallow minds reject and ridicule as they may, the fact remains that there is *no* explanation of the universe, nor of man, apart from the creative genius of GOD.

Remove GOD from the scene and there is neither sense nor reason in the UNIVERSE. Remove MAN and there is neither sense nor reason in CREATION.

—*Alfred A. Montapert*

* * *

QUESTION?

What will I wish, a month, a year, five years, from now that I should have done today?

—*Personal Planning Manual*

★ ★ ★

TO BUILD A MAN

IN OUR AGE WE HAVE LOST THE ART OF BUILDING A MAN. A man is strong in proportion to his ability not only to resist temptation toward unworthy things, but also to desire worthiness. Our character is really nothing but a composite of our impulses, our ambitions, and our tendencies in the direction of right and wrong. There can be nothing more useful or necessary to the individual than a basic philosophy for living, and codes of conduct are usually founded in religious convictions.

—*Alfred A. Montapert*

★ ★ ★

AMERICA, THE LAST HOPE

Today we are going through a revolution. Ideals rooted in the Bible and the classics which have preserved civilization are tossed to the wind. We all want to do our thing. Demagogues come along who appeal to the lowest emotions of the masses. Result ... money becoming worthless, morals and family life at their lowest ebb. Our prosperity is false, as we are buying it. Greed is the name of the losing game. Wake up, America! You are the last hope of the World.

—*Charles W. Miller*

★ ★ ★

CONTRIBUTION

Have you ever thought about and looked about for a means of offering to the world a lasting memorial which should be of some help to humanity?

—*Hal Leighton*

★ ★ ★

DISTRIBUTION

Free enterprise...
    Unequal distribution of blessings.
Socialism...
    Unequal distribution of misery.

—*Winston Churchill*

★ ★ ★

LIBERAL
A liberal is one
Who is driven to do good
With someone else's money.

—*William D. Montapert*

★ ★ ★

BUSINESS

If the spirit of business adventure is killed, this country will cease to hold the foremost position in the world.

—*Andrew W. Mellon*

★ ★ ★

CONSTITUTIONAL RIGHTS

Today many are crying out to keep their rights guaranteed by the Constitution of the United States. These rights do not rest on human institutions, but flow from God. If we wish to keep our rights, we must also keep our God.

—*Bishop Fulton Sheen*

TOO MUCH GIVE-AWAY

Our Government is the BEST in the world
...BUT...
it is getting so BIG it is breaking down.
It is BUYING our prosperity.
It is drowning in DEBT.
It has lost its FINANCIAL responsibility.
It is gradually ERODING the value of our money.
The inevitable RESULT is the PRODUCERS will
not be able to support our Government's
GRANDIOSE "GIVE-AWAY" SCHEMES.

—*Alfred A. Montapert*

★ ★ ★

LEGAL SHYSTERS

It has been my experience that members of the legal profession are contributing substantially to the erosion of values and institutions on which our societies are based. In their quest for money and power, many lawyers seem to have forgotten their obligations.

—*Admiral Hyman G. Rickover*

★ ★ ★

GOOD AND EVIL

The liberals want to take the guns away from the people SO AS TO DISARM THEM—not that they want to lessen crime. They are dealing with an effect, not a first cause.

"I must fight if I would win!" is Nature's dictum down through the centuries. Life is a constant battle between the forces of Good and Evil. Always has been ... always will be.

—*Richard W. Sampson*

★ ★ ★

JUSTICE

The statue of the blindfolded lady JUSTICE with the scale was just fine when they made it. But look what they have done to destroy it! The sword has been removed. Today there is little or no punishment. This protection to the criminals is called human dignity.

But what about the dead victim? The sword was put there to punish the criminals. If the innocent die, why must not the criminals die? Today the so-called "do-gooders" have hidden the sword. When Shakespeare said, *"First shoot all the lawyers,"* I believe he had all the shyster lawyers in mind.

Today, the Sword of Justice has been omitted ... and this symbolizes what I believe to be the chief cause of the disgraceful state of our society.

—*Alfred A. Montapert*

* * *

RIGHT AND WRONG

By what law of right does unrighteousness bring the same consideration as righteousness claims? Righteousness alone will exalt, stabilize and develop a nation.

—*Distilled Wisdom*

* * *

FIRST CAUSES

Our Government has entirely lost the ability to trace effects back to prime first causes. That is why they never get anything fixed.

—*Anthony B. Montapert*

* * *

There's small choice in rotten apples.

—*Shakespeare*

EDUCATION

Billy Graham writes:

"You can put a public school and a university in the middle of every block of every city in America—but you will never keep America from rotting morally by mere intellectual education. Education cannot be properly called education which neglects the most important parts of man's nature. Partial education is far worse than none at all, if we educate the mind but not the soul."

* * *

VALUES

There is NO example in history of a society successfully maintaining any kind of moral life without the aid of religion.

—*William D. Montapert*

* * *

THE AGE OF ANXIETY

We live in a time of unusual insecurity. In the past twenty years so many long-established traditions have broken down—traditions of family life, social life, or the economic order of government and of religious belief. As the years go by, there seems to be so much uncertainty, so much addiction to dope, so much crime.

—*The Supreme Philosophy of Man*

* * *

INDEPENDENCE

Because government assistance usually leads to government interference, all stable and solid organizations steadfastly guard their independence from federal funding. Cities and states continually beg from the government for political favors.

—*Alfred A. Montapert*

* * *

PROGRESS

Men can know more than their ancestors did if they start with a knowledge of what their ancestors had already learned. This is why a society can progress ONLY if it conserves its traditions, then refines and builds.

—*Distilled Wisdom*

* * *

GOD'S VIEWPOINT

From time immemorial, God's problem has been to get men to look from His viewpoint. Man's failure in this particular area is the reason for the condition of the world today.

—*Frederick K. Price*

* * *

A BETTER WORLD

Madame Curie once said: "You cannot hope to build a better world without improving the individuals. To that end, each of us must work for his own improvement and, at the same time, share a general responsibility for all humanity, our particular duty being to aid those to whom we think we can be most useful."

* * *

FOUNDATION FOR LIFE

Life must begin at some point of contact with the Infinite God, whose language is the language of life, and whose fellowship is the meaning of life. LIFE BEGINS AT THE POINT WHERE CONTACT IS MADE WITH FULL ENVIRONMENT. THIS IS THE FOUNDATION FOR ALL SUCCESSFUL LIVING, AND IT IS DEMONSTRATED IN THE LIVES OF ALL INTELLIGENT MEN EVERYWHERE.

—*The Supreme Philosophy of Man*

* * *

COPING IN TODAY'S WORLD

Our problem: everything is on the negative side if you want to be honest. However, each individual reader must raise himself up and not be part of the herd. He must face reality and realize the facts and condition of the world, but he must plan his attitude, life, and investments to cope with the conditions that are facing each one of us today. He must have the "can-do" spirit of a winner.

—*Alfred A. Montapert*

★ ★ ★

RIGHT ATTITUDE

NO ONE can hurt you unless you let them. THERE IS ONE THING OVER WHICH EACH PERSON HAS ABSO-LUTE INHERENT CONTROL, AND THAT IS HIS MENTAL ATTITUDE. NO ONE CAN HURT YOU BUT YOURSELF! LIFE IS MADE OR MARRED BY OUR HABITUAL THINKING.

—*Supreme Philosophy of Man*

★ ★ ★

COPING WITH STRESS

The executive who is under constant pressure from his customers and employees alike; the person who drives the busy freeways, who knows that a moment of distraction may mean death to several people; the athlete who is desperately trying to win a race; the husband who helplessly watches his wife slowly and painfully die of cancer...all suffer from stress. The secret is ADAPTABILITY...Your mind can make or break you!

—*Hans Selye*

★ ★ ★

WHAT SHALL WE DO?

If all these adverse conditions did not exist I would not need my Hall of Wisdom. BUT in order to cope with the present conditions of today's world, WE NEED INSPIRATION AND MOTIVATION and all the brains we can borrow.

These ideas constitute a dynamic library of words to live by, motivations to action, inspiration, and courage to face life's daily battles.

It is my humble hope that some of these sayings will help you to cope in today's world—help by giving you guidelines to live by, encouragement to keep fighting when everything around you seems to be falling apart. Maybe they will give you a smile or two to brighten the dark times, the insights to help make the suffering bearable, and inspiration to enrich your life.

I am sharing my Wealth with you. It is up to YOU to benefit by it.

—*Alfred A. Montapert*

* * *

THE LAST TIME

Some day you will use your tools or lock your desk for the last time. You will put away your working equipment, and 999 chances out of a thousand you will not know it is for the last time. Some day you will say your last prayer. You may not know it is the last time. You may be like the soldier fatally wounded who started his prayer, but never finished it. I stood for a long time in the doorway of my office, reluctant to leave it, for the last time.

—*Alfred A. Montapert*

* * *

TODAY

This is the beginning of a fresh new day,
    I greet it with HOPE.
Today comes only once, and never again returns,
    I must show my LOVE and be KIND.
God has given me this 24 hours to use as I will,
    I shall have a cheerful ATTITUDE.
I must do something GOOD with this day and not waste it.
This is my day of opportunity and duty, I expect something
    GOOD because I am going to help make it happen!

Today is a NEW DAY in my LIFE, a new piece of road to be
    traveled; I must ask God for directions.
Today I will be filled with courage and confidence;
    I must show my FAITH in God.
What I do today is very important because I am exchanging a
    day of MY LIFE for it.
The COST of a thing is the amount of MY LIFE
    I spend obtaining it.

When tomorrow comes, this day will be gone forever,
    leaving in its place something I have traded for it.
In order not to forget the price I paid for it, I shall do my best
    to make it USEFUL, PROFITABLE, JOYFUL.
The seeds I plant today determine my HARVEST in the
    future; my life will be RICHER OR POORER by the way
    I use today.
Thank you, God, for today; I shall not pass this way again—
    What I must do, I'll do today!

—Alfred A. Montapert

★ ★ ★

ACT

My son, now that thou knowest and hast read all these
things, happy shalt thou be if thou do them.

—Thomas A. Kempis

★ ★ ★